RECONSIDERING AMERICAN POLITICAL THOUGHT

Filling in the missing spaces left by traditional textbooks on American political thought, *Reconsidering American Political Thought* uses race, gender, and ethnicity as a lens through which to engage ongoing debates on American values and intellectual traditions. Weaving document-based texts analysis with short excerpts from classics in American literature, this book presents a re-examination of the political and intellectual debates of consequence throughout American history.

Purposely beginning the story in 1619, Saladin Ambar reassesses the religious, political, and social histories of the colonial period in American history. Thereafter, Ambar moves through the story of America, with each chapter focusing on a different era in American history up to the present day. Ambar threads together analysis of periods including Thomas Jefferson's aspiration to create an "Empire of Liberty," the ethnic, racial, and gender-based discourse instrumental in creating a "Yankee" industrial state between 1877 and 1932, and the intellectual, cultural, and social forces that led to the political rise of Ronald Reagan and Barack Obama in recent decades. In closing, Ambar assesses the prospects for a new, more invigorated political thought and discourse to reshape and redirect national energies and identity in the Trump presidency.

Reconsidering American Political Thought presents a broad and subjective view about critical arguments in American political thought, giving future generations of students and lecturers alike an inclusive understanding of how to teach, research, study, and think about American political thought.

Saladin Ambar is Associate Professor of Political Science and Senior Scholar at the Center on the American Governor at the Eagleton Institute of Politics at Rutgers University–New Brunswick. He is the author of *How Governors Built the Modern American Presidency* (University of Pennsylvania Press, 2012) and *Malcolm X at Oxford Union: Racial Politics in a Global Era* (Oxford University Press, 2014), which was nominated for a Hurston/Wright Legacy Award for best non-fiction book by an African American author. Ambar's most recent book, *American Cicero: Mario Cuomo and the Defense of American Liberalism* (Oxford University Press, 2017), is the first to examine the entire political career of former New York Governor Mario M. Cuomo. Ambar's research interests include the American presidency, American political development, American political thought, and race and ethnic politics.

"Scholars, students, and everyone else seeking to understand US political thought will be swept up by Saladin Ambar's retelling of the American story. *Reconsidering American Political Thought* is populated by a familiar cast of characters and yet is refreshing and original in its recentering of figures whose voices have been erased or relegated to footnotes in similar texts. Ambar's writing sparkles, his editorial choices are incisive, and the narrative his text spins from these choices soars."

Elizabeth F. Cohen, *Professor of Political Science, Maxwell School of Citizenship and Public Affairs, Syracuse University*

"Composed with clarity and verve, this refreshingly inclusive treatment of American political thought places race and gender at the center, from which they had been marginalized far too long. By inviting students into the realm of ideas as shaping, and shaped by, historical development, the book offers a deep reconsideration and a model of learned revision."

Ira I. Katznelson, *Ruggles Professor of Political Science and History, Columbia University*

"Saladin Ambar's work, *Reconsidering American Political Thought,* is an impressive weaving together of variegated strands of four centuries of American political thinking and understanding. This book is able to do something that is quite rare: putting all facets of political thought into sustained dialogue and positioning that dialogue within a nuanced and inclusive understanding of American political history and development. This is a brilliant, thoughtful, and deeply researched exploration of not only American political thought, but ultimately what that thought teaches about the people, the governmental system, and the future of this vast continent."

Lilly J. Goren, *Professor of Political Science, Carroll University, Waukesha, WI*

"A dazzling book that reconsiders America itself. Ambar broadens our gaze by adding race and gender perspectives to the great sweep of American thinking. He broadens it further by placing literature, history, religion, and national myth alongside the familiar thinkers. The result is a bold, essential, elegant, fascinating, fresh, subversive way to read the United States and its peoples."

James A. Morone, *John Hazen White Professor of Political Science, Public Policy, and Urban Studies, Brown University*

"Ideas jump off the page in this beautifully written and artfully conceived text of political theory written for all of us. Starting from a different vantage point, Ambar conveys with flair the continuing relevance of political theory in diverse democracy."

Jane Yunhee Junn, *Professor of Political Science, USC*

RECONSIDERING AMERICAN POLITICAL THOUGHT

A New Identity

Saladin Ambar

Routledge
Taylor & Francis Group

NEW YORK AND LONDON

First published 2020
by Routledge
52 Vanderbilt Avenue, New York, NY 10017

and by Routledge
2 Park Square, Milton Park, Abingdon, Oxon, OX14 4RN

Routledge is an imprint of the Taylor & Francis Group, an informa business

© 2020 Taylor & Francis

Library of Congress Cataloging-in-Publication Data
Names: Ambar, Saladin M., author.
Title: Reconsidering American political thought : a new identity / Saladin Ambar.
Description: New York, NY : Routledge, 2020. | Includes bibliographical references and index.
Identifiers: LCCN 2019043539 (print) | LCCN 2019043540 (ebook) | ISBN 9781138341722 (hardback) | ISBN 9781138343894 (paperback) | ISBN 9780429438837 (ebook) | ISBN 9780429798191 (adobe pdf) | ISBN 9780429798177 (mobi) | ISBN 9780429798184 (epub)
Subjects: LCSH: Political science—United States—History. | United States—Politics and government.
Classification: LCC JA84.U5 .A67 2020 (print) | LCC JA84.U5 (ebook) | DDC 320.0973—dc23
LC record available at https://lccn.loc.gov/2019043539
LC ebook record available at https://lccn.loc.gov/2019043540

ISBN: 978-1-138-34172-2 (hbk)
ISBN: 978-1-138-34389-4 (pbk)
ISBN: 978-0-429-43883-7 (ebk)

Typeset in Galliard
by Swales & Willis, Exeter, Devon, UK

This book is dedicated to public school teachers everywhere, and
In memory of the historian John Pettegrew

CONTENTS

Introduction		1
Chapter One	Colonial Legacies: 1619–1763	9
Chapter Two	Revolution and Order: 1763–1800	31
Chapter Three	Jefferson's "Empire of Liberty": 1800–1850	53
Chapter Four	Fracture and Reunion: 1850–1877	79
Chapter Five	Political Thought and the New American State: 1877–1932	103
Chapter Six	Redefining Rights: 1932–1980	125
Chapter Seven	Neoconservatism and Superpower: 1980–2018	149
Index		*169*

INTRODUCTION

When I was asked to consider writing a new textbook in American political thought, I was at once excited and, admittedly, somewhat daunted. I had not to that point written a large work in the field of political theory. And although my work has been consciously theory-laden, I was squarely in the sub-discipline of American political development, having written a historical work on the presidency, a micro-history of Malcolm X, and a political biography of former New York Governor Mario Cuomo. When I sat down with the Acquisitions Editor for a publisher later subsumed under Routledge to discuss what I might have in mind, I was happily convinced that this book could contribute something of consequence to students of American politics who were in need of a different approach to the topic. That conversation led to a second, longer discussion with Natalja Mortensen, the current Senior Acquisitions Editor at Routledge, who has been responsible for shepherding this book to the finish line in a form better than it was at the start. Thankfully, Natalja saw great value in the project, and was exceedingly patient with me through a variety of fits and stops as I plodded along. Her talent, warmth, and generous spirit were invaluable to me.

Ultimately, our conversations were about a single question: What would make a new book in American political thought worthwhile? For that, I had only to ponder my own undergraduate experience, where, when studying political philosophy at Georgetown University – and struggling mightily, I might add – I recognized only many years later what might have made those courses more engaging for me as an 18-year-old black kid from Queens, the son of an Italian American mother who had been on and off welfare, making a better life for herself and family in the Reagan Era of "Morning in America."

That revelation came when researching for my book on Malcolm X's speech at Oxford in 1964. I learned, somewhat haphazardly, that Malcolm X was very fond of the German philosopher G.W.F. Hegel, a thinker whose work as an undergraduate I was introduced to, but was dumbfounded over. Had I known Malcolm's "House Negro–Field Negro" illustration of black life in America had been very much wed to Hegel's master–slave dialectic, I might have been drawn in. Which is a roundabout way of saying it is the hope of this book that students from all walks of life might find avenues of entry for thinking about American political thought anew, or even for the first time – because they can see themselves in it. Making this possible involved three commitments – and thankfully, Natalja and Routledge were excited about sharing them with me.

The first need was to place this book at the intersection of race and gender, making it not a textbook "incorporating" those critical variables in American life, but rather, truly foregrounding them in the writing, as much as they are foregrounded in the history and lives of the American people. Indeed, Routledge had already produced a textbook covering race and gender *thematically* (along with radical and conservative ideologies).[1] But to date, there is no text in American political thought that takes a historical approach (as most textbooks in American political thought do) while at the same time directly addressing race and gender as critical features of the historical narrative (which most do not), rather than as a subset of a "larger story."

Second, this could not be a "textbook" in the strictest sense of the word. It would not, and does not, offer a panoply of writings and other documents essential to such books. Instead, this text would be a companion to those more traditional works – to be read by students as a second voice along with documents and commentaries provided by their faculty. This book is thus better understood as offering a series of essays speaking to those otherwise more traditional works in American political thought – a kind of shadow, to borrow a metaphor from the novelist Ralph Ellison, that would engage, prompt – maybe even shame, dare I say – future texts into seeking a more central place for the voices of women, blacks, indigenous peoples, and other marginalized groups in their narratives. As a companion, it is meant to provoke greater discussion of the ideologies and thinkers found in American political thought – while also providing an inherent critique of how that intellectual history is often presented to us. Given its approachable length, it is my hope that students will find it a helpful (and manageable) accompaniment to the intellectual history they are being asked to grapple with.

No book can accomplish all the comprehensiveness, detail, and readability required for a single course in American political thought. But that is a straw man argument. Where shortcomings are present, they should be acknowledged – and I wish to do so now. While race and gender are richly interwoven into the narrative of the book, my research and analysis of gender are not as strong as that of race. This is not so much an apologia for a book whose presentation of gender in the field of American political thought I view as comparatively strong; it is nevertheless a signal to faculty and students alike to be conscious readers in formulating theory-based questions and approaches that add greater dimension to the history that I've covered with respect to gender.

That brings me to this book's historical approach. It is an old saw that we need to engage in a broader and more inclusive politics, "now, more than ever." Yet Seyla Benhabib was right, nearly 20 years ago, when she presciently wrote about the value of political theory today. "We can expect that in the next couple of decades," she wrote, "significant constitutional issues will emerge in the wake of the deterritorialization of politics." She added, "[C]ompelling answers to these problems will require not only normative theory but a hybrid mode that draws on historical-institutional analysis."[2] This is certainly true in the case of American politics – and this book is therefore an effort to meld historical analysis to theory. Placing our current political challenges (especially those driven by racial and gender differences) – including those in American political thought – in historical context offers the most effective route to understanding their origins in theory and in practice.

The final commitment Routledge and I agreed to was to expand the horizon of what constitutes American political thought by culling more openly from the American literary tradition. Given that there is great debate, even now, about what constitutes American philosophy, it is clear, at least to me, that the political thought of the United States has always been richly informed, and on occasion pushed politically, by the voices of its writers. This is undoubtedly also so for its artists, poets, and musicians, though I've been less rash in thinking I could incorporate them effectively as well – though in my conclusion, I end this text with allusions to the words of Bob Dylan and Robert Frost. I hope other scholars, more effectively equipped than I, will go further.

My academic training in political theory has occurred at three excellent but very different institutions. In short, Jesuits, Marxists, and civic republicans trained me. At Georgetown, I learned as much from my Theology professors about political thought as I did from my professors in Philosophy. The late Fr. Lawrence Madden, SJ (The Problem of God) and Fr. James Schall, SJ (Introduction to Biblical Literature) were magnificent at drawing out the political from the spiritual – and helping me see the power of faith in the American political experience. They have passed on, and I wish to thank them posthumously here.

That allusion to Marxists, however tongue-in-cheek, refers to my time at the New School for Social Research – whose Graduate Faculty was established as a University in Exile in the 1930s for Jews and other intellectuals fleeing the reaches of Nazism and fascism. At the New School I encountered the late Jacob Landynski and other extraordinary professors, including Richard Bensel and Ira Katznelson. Their teaching opened me up to how political thought shapes, and is in turn shaped by, the historical experience. I got a far greater richness and depth in historical analysis at the New School than I thought possible. It was an amazing time for a student in his early twenties to be at the Graduate Faculty with access to such marvelous scholars.

Finally, my civic republican allusion is a reference to my short but deeply moving experience as one of the many students of the great Wilson Carey McWilliams, who could write about Ralph Waldo Emerson and the far more obscure but highly significant writer Harold Cruse (the author of The Crisis of the Negro Intellectual), with equal aplomb. My exposure to McWilliams' writings, and more importantly, his teaching – and even more importantly, his love for his students – has placed me in a position of deep gratitude for a classroom experience I still have not shaken. With Dan Tichenor as my dissertation adviser and friend at Rutgers, I came to learn how to think and write less as a graduate student, and more as a scholar. I could not have been more fortunate to be shaped by these individuals and these institutions.

But I want to offer one more note of thanks before moving on to the descriptive part of this Introduction. It is a long overdue note of thanks to my high school honors English teacher, Joan Pinto, and really, for the dozens of public school teachers I've had in my life. It was Mrs. Pinto who introduced me most forthrightly to a life of the mind – who treated me – dare I say it? – like an intellectual as a 16-year-old. She had no business doing that at John Bowne High School in Flushing, New York. But she did – and many thousands of America's public school teachers do so, with little to no fanfare or reward. This book is dedicated to them. It was in front of a classroom, after all, where I truly learned American political history and the thought that shaped it. For nearly 20 years, I taught American History in the public schools of New York and New Jersey. It was the most rewarding professional experience of my life – and I'd like to honor my fellow teachers and colleagues by drawing attention to their labor. They remain my heroes in many ways, and we as a nation must do better by them.

Reconsidering American Political Thought

American political thought, perhaps unlike other academic approaches to political and intellectual history, engages a form of connectedness, if not love, for its subject than is customary. Being an "Americanist" in political science is often associated with a kind of conservative or less critical posture at times – and being an American political theorist is often the right root of this branch. But this is ultimately a facile proposition – at least when viewing America's intellectual history critically. The need to "reconsider" American political thought has to do with ensuring that any analysis of the thinkers identified (and those who perhaps should be) with this tradition is not erased of their association with race and gender – be it a positive association or otherwise.

A new identity for American political thought is needed for a new citizenry – one whose investigation of the past will be increasingly informed by the political reality of a more empowered women's status within the body politic, and a social milieu moving towards a majority "minority" republic. These two transformations alone warrant not so much a revisionist approach to American intellectual history, but a corrective of the tendency to isolate, negate, or ignore the dynamic role of race and gender in shaping the contours of American life. And while I have not signaled class as a critical feature within the text, I have placed great stress on its undeniable role in influencing both race and gender relations – and every chief undercurrent of American politics.

This companion takes a consciously historical approach, beginning in 1619 and moving towards the present. Such breadth cannot encompass all the important thinkers and movements within American political thought. My hope is that readers will adopt the disposition of one visiting a museum – this wing represents a limited but critical range of the historical narrative. Even if it were the equivalent of the Elgin Marbles (and that it hardly is), one wouldn't stop there in pursuit of understanding Ancient Greece. My hope is that the piece fits within the essential history, providing insights that would be forsaken had one not made the detour. We need more works, not fewer, to round out what has been an uneven field. This book does not finish that job; in many ways, we are just beginning.

In Chapter One I purposely begin the course in 1619, the year the first Africans arrived in Jamestown. The presumption is, that American political thought has mostly insisted that there are one or two intellectual foundings in American history – the Pilgrim and Puritan landings in 1620 or 1630. By beginning the text with American slavery, students are forced to reconsider the religious, political, and social histories of the colonial period – including the first Anglo interactions with Native Americans. The focus is on the interactions between race, gender, and class relations in the New World.

In the second chapter I examine the movement from a more radical, revolutionary political ethos in the United States towards one grounded in order. The focus is on how American thinkers and political actors authored and responded to the push for republican government, while at once attempting to re-order notions of liberty along racial lines.

Chapter Three follows up with a discussion and review of Thomas Jefferson's aspiration to create an "Empire of Liberty" after the purchase of the Louisiana Territory. Here I place the emphasis on what this "empire" established for indigenous peoples, blacks, and women.

In Chapter Four I explore the period of political disintegration, secession, war, and reunion. The chapter focuses on the role of violence in shaping national politics, and how America's constitutional reordering after the Civil War was fraught with challenges rooted in the nation's racial identity.

This is followed by Chapter Five's focus on the ethnic, racial, and gender-based discourse instrumental in creating a "Yankee" industrial state, comprised of many different groups, in the period after Reconstruction. Discussion includes an examination of the role of political thought in establishing notions of belonging, with examples covering the Chinese Exclusion Act (1882), the Spanish–American War (1898), and women's suffrage (1920).

In Chapter Six I explore FDR's New Deal politics and new theories of economic justice. The rise and fall of America's liberal state is the theme, with critical transformations in immigration, the social status of women, and the black freedom struggle also part of a narrative evaluating contending intellectual and ideological strands of thought, including the rise of modern conservatism. The final chapter, Chapter Seven, encompasses a discussion of the political rise of Ronald Reagan and Barack Obama, placing in context the intellectual, cultural, and social forces that led to each historic presidency. With the rise of America as the world's Superpower after the fall of the Soviet Union, the chapter places in context both neoliberalism and neoconservatism's attempts to navigate a world where American leadership and democratic virtues have been deeply called into question, particularly after September 11, 2001. I close with an assessment of the present state of American political thought, taking into account the strains on conservatism and liberalism alike, in the Trump presidency. What are the prospects for new, more invigorated political thought and discourse to reshape and redirect national energies and identity?

This book could not have been written without support and feedback from my colleagues. I'd especially like to thank the Director of the Eagleton Institute of Politics at Rutgers University, Ruth Mandel, who supported, in both funding and good cheer, my writing this book. I'd likewise like to thank colleagues who read various chapters and/or provided specific feedback and encouragement. While too many to name, I'd be remiss if I didn't single out the help of Carol Nackenoff, Paul

Frymer, and Jeffrey Tulis. Lastly, I wish to thank my friend and department chair, Rick Lau at Rutgers University–New Brunswick, who encouraged my undertaking this project from the very beginning.

Writing is an inherently solitary enterprise, and it takes the energy, love, and support of friends and loved ones to pull one through. For this, I am grateful beyond expression for the love of my children Gabrielle, Luke, and Daniel. It was a moment with them some years ago, at the Cherokee Heritage Center in Talhequah, Oklahoma, when Luke taught me the finest distinction to be made when critiquing the historic actions of one's country. While sharing with them the story of the Trail of Tears, I kept pointing out how "We removed the Indian tribes from their lands, pushing Native Americans further west." Nearly every sentence began with "We did such and so." Finally, Luke had had enough. All of six years old, he looked up at me and said:

"Dad, don't say 'we.' Say, 'the Government.'"

And now I have.

Saladin Ambar
New Brunswick, NJ
May, 2019

Notes

1. Jonathan Keller and Alex Zamalin, *American Political Thought: An Alternative View* (New York: Routledge, 2017).
2. See Seyla Benhabib, "Political Theory and Political Membership in a Changing World," in Ira Katznelson and Helen V. Milner (Eds.), *Political Science: State of the Discipline* (pp. 404–432) (New York: W.W. Norton, 2002).

CHAPTER ONE
COLONIAL LEGACIES: 1619–1763

Introduction

The French historian Ernest Renan famously remarked in a lecture at the Sorbonne in Paris in 1888 that "Forgetting, I would even say historical error, is an essential factor in the creation of a nation." His reasoning was that "[T]he progress of historical studies often poses a threat to nationality" (Renan, 251, 2018). America's colonial origins and legacy have invited any number of such strategic lapses in memory. Yet determining the circumstances of America's birth shouldn't be so contentious. That is, if we are to presume that the United States of America, unlike other nations, can be said to have been conceived intentionally, as Alexander Hamilton argued in *The Federalist* (Hamilton, Jay, and Madison, 1788), then its origins can be documented. In *Federalist* No. 1, Hamilton asked whether "societies of men are really capable or not of establishing government from reflection or choice, or whether they are forever destined to depend for their political constitutions on accident and force."[1]

For Hamilton, the answer was that the American Constitution of 1787 marked the point of conception of nationhood. In making this case, he was occluding the violence of the recent and more distant past: the Revolutionary War that gave independence to the American colonies, and the wars waged by Anglo-American settlers against the indigenous peoples they encountered. This was the "force" left unaccounted for in Hamilton's argument to replace the Articles of Confederation; and it is very much the type of "forgetting" Renan had in mind in his speech 100 years after the Constitution was ratified.

Of course, Renan was not directing his remarks to Americans. He was more interested in critiquing the nationalism evidenced on his side of the Atlantic in the late nineteenth century. But his words remain instructive about national identity – perhaps none more so than for Americans, who often pride themselves on a nationality of democratic virtue rather than one derived from blood. Yet, even when accepting the premise that the United States is a nation created by democratic thought, deciding where to trace the origins of national birth can be a tricky affair. Part of the magic of the Gettysburg Address lies in Abraham Lincoln's leapfrogging over the Constitution (and its acceptance of slavery) to the Declaration of Independence. Those "four score and seven years ago" brought Lincoln's 1863 audience to 1776 and Thomas Jefferson's words – "All men are created equal." The new birth of freedom Lincoln sought was to be a second iteration of liberty – with the difference being a liberty untainted by the scourge of slavery. As the historian Garry Wills has pointed out, the Declaration's purity on the slave question made it a safe landing spot for Lincoln in reimagining America's national origins (Wills, 1992).

But this is just the beginning of debates about the "true" origins of American national identity. It was another Frenchman, Alexis de Tocqueville, who argued in his groundbreaking work *Democracy in America* (originally published in French in 1835) that American national origins go well beyond either its Constitution or Declaration. In fact, Tocqueville never bothered to mention the Declaration of Independence in his great work. How can this be?

As the political scientist James W. Ceaser has noted, Tocqueville was engaging in his own sleight of hand. *Democracy in America* leapfrogged not only the Constitution and Declaration of Independence, but also the entire history of the Enlightenment in American history (Ceaser, 2011). Instead, Tocqueville placed America's political origins at the Puritan founding, seeing in its New England Protestant beginnings the seeds of democratic ideals to come. This choice contained another form of forgetting, however. In opting to begin what he called the "point of depart-ure" for American national identity in New England, Tocqueville made a conscious choice to deemphasize the Virginian founding moment. This third strategic leapfrog saw in the Massachusetts Pil-grim landing at Plymouth in 1620 something of greater conse-quence than the "other" Pilgrim landing at Jamestown in 1607. Tocqueville was careful to explain his selection:

> In the great Anglo-American family one can distinguish two principal offshoots that, up to the present, have grown without being entirely confused, one in the South, the other in the North. Virginia received the first English colony. The emigrants arrived there in 1607. Europe at that time was still singularly preoccupied with the idea that gold and silver mines made the wealth of peoples: a fatal idea that has more than impoverished the European nations that gave themselves to it and destroyed more men in America than have war and all bad laws together .... No noble thought, no immaterial scheme presided at the foundation of the new settlements. Hardly had the colony been created when they introduced slavery; that was the capital fact that was bound to exert an immense influence on the character, the laws, and the whole future of the South.
>
> (Tocqueville, 30–31, 2000)

Thus, as Lincoln elected to choose the Declaration over the Constitu-tion for his founding moment, so too did Tocqueville selectively advance one national narrative over another. The founders of James-town and the American South became subordinate to those of New England and the North – primarily on account of their vested interest in slavery. New England ideals were the ones Tocqueville chose to see as most influential. "The civilization of New England," he wrote, in one of his more literary passages, "has been like those fires lit in the hills that, after having spread heat around them, still tinge the furthest reaches of the horizon with their light" (Tocqueville, 32).

New England exceptionalism thus became the first form of Ameri-can exceptionalism. The choice to reject the Jamestown founding advanced a number of important ideas that still prevail in American political thought. The first is that the United States as a country has been fundamentally egalitarian in its ethos from the start – a point that the political scientist Rogers Smith among others, has sought to challenge (Smith, 1999). The second idea is that American slavery was essentially a southern rather than a national phenomenon. In choosing 1620 over 1607, Tocqueville's founding premise marginalized the influence of slavery over national political development – and with it, its influence over American political thought. Finally, in rejecting Jamestown's significance, in exchange for a "cleaner" version of national identity, we are left without the story of slavery and indentured servitude's influence on early American history – and more fundamentally, the Anglo-American relationship with those indigenous tribes and nations they encountered.

It was, after all, the interlocking connection between slavery, English expansion, and the privileging of white settlement that made the presence of Native Americans untenable for the first English colonizers, and those to come. It is for this reason that we may more properly begin the story of the rise of American political thought in 1619, the year the first 20 Africans were brought to Jamestown as enslaved persons. This is not to idealize the African contribution to American history over others. On the contrary, it is to emphasize that neither New England nor Virginia can lay claim to any "pure" American founding. No such founding exists. We are closer to the mark to choose an intermediary moment – one that implicates race and the portent of Indian removal – for it is that feature that, despite heroic attempts to hide it, most illuminates the complex array of social, political, and economic bases that undergirded the earliest political thought of the colonial period. W.E.B. Du Bois was right to remind his readers in *The Souls of Black Folks*, "Before the Pilgrims landed we [blacks] were here" (Du Bois, 162, 1999). But before the arrival of either group, there was a rich and formidable world of indigenous life in North America. And any consideration of American political thought must abide this most basic of facts.

Indigenous History and the Myth of a New Eden

For readers who might not have been paying attention, F. Scott Fitzgerald ended his greatest novel by invoking the American republic and its origins. Describing the once bucolic surrounding areas of his protagonists' home, Fitzgerald reminded his audience that *The Great Gatsby* is in fact about America and its deepest meaning. The word "republic" is a clumsy word for a literary work, but it somehow fit nicely into Fitzgerald's closing argument – both stylistically and historically. The United States is a dream, perhaps an at times ugly or even misdirected dream, but a dream nonetheless. And the dream of America's republic, like Gatsby's vision of love, is one founded upon falsehoods and unattainable longings. So, for its evocation of a barren, Edenic land ready for conquest and to be "tamed," it is worth returning to *The Great Gatsby* to consider the endurance of that most primordial of national myths – an empty continent – and to contemplate its historic value. Here is how Fitzgerald ends his novel:

> And as the moon rose higher the inessential houses began to melt away until gradually I became aware of the old island here that flowered once for Dutch sailors' eyes – a fresh, green breast of the new world. Its vanished trees, the trees that had made the way for Gatsby's house, had once pandered in whispers to the last and greatest of all human dreams; for a transitory enchanted moment man must have held his breath in the presence of this continent, compelled into an aesthetic contemplation he neither understood nor desired, face to face for the last time in history with something commensurate to his capacity for wonder …. He did not know that it was already behind him, somewhere back in that vast obscurity beyond the city, where the dark fields of the republic rolled on under the night.
>
> (Fitzgerald, 180, 2004)

There are few passages in American literature as elegant or as stridently hagiographic as this one. In presenting to us the "old island," the "fresh, green breast of the new world," and "the vanished trees," Fitzgerald is offering us an uninhabited, pristine, idyllic New York – truly an unbesmirched "continent." It is moving and sweeping in its descriptiveness. And, it is a narrative that completely ignores the presence of millions of indigenous people who called this continent home.

There were people here.

As the historian William Cronon noted, there were somewhere between 70,000 and 100,000 indigenous people living in New England alone around 1600. It took 100 years before the European population of New England reached this number in 1700 (Cronon, 42, 2003). Aside from encountering people, the first European settlers also encountered a land that had been clearly managed, cultivated, and transformed by human hands. As Charles Mann wrote in *1491: New Revelations of the Americas before Columbus*:

> Constant burning of undergrowth [by Native Americans] increased the numbers of herbivores, the predators that fed on them, and the people who ate them both. Rather than the thick, unbroken, monumental snarl of trees imagined by [Henry David] Thoreau, the great eastern forest was an ecological kaleidoscope of garden plots, blackberry rambles, pine barrens, and spacious groves of chestnut, hickory, and oak.
>
> (Mann, 286, 2011)

Indian influence on the environment also included the creation of "paths of indigenous fires," allowing for a migratory trail of bison from New York to Georgia (Mann, 286). With the addition of a well-managed system of roads created by Native Americans that extended throughout the continent, America was hardly a "virgin" territory, a term more in keeping with the value system of European patriarchy than historical reality. As Roxanne Dunbar-Ortiz concluded in her study, *An Indigenous Peoples' History of the United States*, "North America in 1492 was not a virgin wilderness but a network of Indigenous nations, people of the corn" (Dunbar-Ortiz, 30, 2014). This matters because the earliest forms of American political thought engage notions of a political community, property rights, and forms of exceptionalism that imagine the United States' political formation as blessed by an enormous, largely uninhabited land, ready to be cultivated and populated by European hands.

Fitzgerald's closing narrative in *Gatsby* is more about an aesthetics of the American imagination than an intentional misdirection of the nation's founding. But it is tied to a long line of more egregious occlusions of indigenous history and colonial violence. In her study of whiteness, Valerie Babb notes the significance of Cotton Mather's purposeful erasure of Native American history. As a highly influential theologian and Puritan thinker, Mather's sermons and writings were a critical part of the formation of early American political thought. As Babb writes about Mather's 1702 work, *Magnalia Christi Americana*:

Mather reiterated for a new generation the myth of Puritan pilgrims coming to the New World; but his flourishes began to racialize this enterprise, as evident in his description of a plague that decimated much of New England's Native American population prior to English arrival.

(Babb, 64, 1998)

Here, Babb cites from the *Magnalia*:

Whereas the good Hand of God now brought [the English] to a Country wonderfully prepared for their Entertainment, by a sweeping Mortality that had lately been among the Natives .... The *Indians* in those Parts had newly, even about a Year or Two before, been visited with such a prodigious Pestilence; as carried away not a *Tenth*, but *Nine Parts of Ten* (yea, 'tis said *Nineteen of Twenty*) among them: So that the Woods were almost cleared of those pernicious Creatures to make Room for a *better Growth*.

(Babb, 64)

Such literary forms of ethnic cleansing became part and parcel of the earliest examples of American exceptionalism, marking America as uniquely situated for greatness. While Mather's sermon "A Christian at His Calling" (1701) is often included in seminal texts in American political thought, his *Magnalia* speaks as forcefully to the emergent gospel of race as his *Calling* does to emergent American Protestantism. The two go hand-in-hand in their construction of a distinctively American ethos during the colonial era. As James A. Morone has written, "The Indians offered English colonists an irreducible, satanic other – perfect for defining the Christian community" (Morone, 74, 2003). The earliest colonial wars were waged in New England and Virginia against Native Americans who quickly fit into the emerging conception of racial groups developing in Europe. The term "race" itself first made its way into a dictionary in 1606, the year before the Jamestown founding – a distinct, yet historically relevant development (Kendi, 36, 2016).

Puritan religious and political thought was affected by the presence of people they took to be innately different from them. "The colonists' doubts about their own identity were magnified by their distance from England and their nearness to the Indians," Jill Lepore has written

(Lepore, 6, 1999). Such doubts were premised upon the question of whether or not the assumed "savagery" of the Indians was owing to their migration from either Europe or Asia, or if they were the products of the land itself, a group resulting from the polygenetic creation of man – an offshoot of sorts – but one whose conditioning in the woods of North America made them somehow susceptible to barbarism (Lepore, 6). The result: "Instead of being the stage for the perfection of piety, the woods of New England might in truth be a forest of depravity" (Lepore, 6).

For example, the English war against the Pequot in New England was especially vicious. Beginning in 1636, it led to their virtual decimation as a group. Cotton Mather chronicled the burning to death of hundreds at a Pequot village (Fort Mystic in Connecticut), during the decisive battle of the war in 1637. "In a little more than an hour," he wrote, "five or six hundred of these barbarians were dismissed from a world that was burdened with them" (Morone, 77–78). For Lepore, the need to distinguish English from Spanish brutality (and Indian barbarism) became the earliest departure for establishing English identity in the colonies. This distinction arose during King Philip's War (1675–1676), although that conflict may said to have been the denouement of a century's long process. Literary scholars and historians alike have long been keen to note that Herman Melville set his ill-fated crew's voyage in *Moby-Dick* upon a ship named for the people who were slaughtered centuries before: the Pequod Indians. It was a name implicating an irony his mid-nineteenth-century readers were far more likely to be attuned to than more contemporary ones.

The Seeds of Colonial Thought

The English settlers in America were dissenters from the great modern dissent movement of Protestantism. Puritan thought was therefore rooted in a restricted sense of belonging – while simultaneously advocating a breakaway philosophy of freethinking on received (Anglican) religious doctrine. The impulse to found a society premised upon new but circumscribed thinking made New England's Puritan communities particularly restrictive. As James A. Morone put it, the Puritan founding was at once a "story of clashing American impulses: inclusion and exclusion, internal grace and external force, toleration and repression" (Morone, 73). The proto-social contract implicit in John Winthrop's "City Upon a Hill" speech aboard the *Arbella* in 1630 (properly known as "A Modell of Christian Charity") argues for a Christian love that binds believers together in both times of plenty and sacrifice: "We must be willing to abridge ourselves of our superfluities, for the supply of other's necessities" (Whittington, 60, 2017). The communal demands encompassed in Winthrop's thought were just that – but what of those outside of the community?

Indians, Quakers, and women within the Puritan community were all outsiders of one type or another on a scale of rights and communal authority. Framing this narrative has proven uneasy at best. Walter McDougall's early American history, for example, removes intentionality from American political thought when it trespasses into unseemly questions tied to the early exercise of English power in America. "English colonists did not come to America intent on killing, enslaving, or for the most part converting or consorting with Indians at all," he writes. "They just wanted them out of the way, and thanks to their microbes, technology, organization, and agriculture, they swiftly displaced the indigenous people in what amounted to a Darwinian contest for an ecological niche" (McDougall, 40, 2004).

Such odes to "accidental" history belie the pre-colonial American history of England's colonization of Ireland and Christian crusader wars against "others" that were the precursors for indigenous displacement and genocide in the New World. Indeed, there is a great deal of violence buried in historical musings of English intentions in the New World ("just wanting them [Native Americans] out of the way"). The brutality of English colonization was part of a historic process that had antecedents in Ireland, if not earlier. As Audrey Horning notes, "Ireland, with its longstanding continental cultural and religious connections, was an unlikely practice ground for the colonization of the Americas, yet its history became intertwined with that of colonial America" (Horning, 16, 2017).

Horning and others are right to emphasize that the English encounter with the other was not as novel as we are often asked to believe. James Morone made a plea of sorts against this traditional theory of American political history when writing about the Puritans:

There's another way to read the Indian conflicts, a different precedent for future American generations. The Puritan-Indian wars were

like conflicts with a foreign power. Some ministers – we would probably call them doves – preached peace, religious conversion, and
even a kind of integration (at least into the praying villages). But the
official epic imagined conflict between God and Satan, good and
evil. The colonists marched and fought as agents of goodness, as the
soldiers of God. The pattern of course, reaches back to the Crusades.
What is distinctively American may be the ambiguity of the crusade,
the flight of both doves and hawks, the debate about whether to
integrate – or fight. Recall the Pequot cries as the boats approached
them: Are you here for trade or for war?

(Morone, 96–97)

Englishness had long been the basis for belonging, certainly before the
Americas – with Puritan religious doctrine its early creed in New England. Roger Williams and Anne Hutchinson's dissent from the dissent-
ing Puritans was the first crack in the essentialism of religious thought
in New England. The anti-Indian, Quaker, and woman bases of Puritanism in America was later directly and indirectly memorialized in
American literature.

Nathaniel Hawthorne's 1835 short story "Young Goodman
Brown" is explicit in its revisionism of American exceptionalism,
a well-trodden myth, even then. "I helped your grandfather, the
constable, when he lashed the Quaker woman … and it was I that
brought your father a pitch-pine knot, kindled at my own hearth, to
set fire to an Indian village in King Philip's war," the Devil tells
Goodman Brown, a well-respected member of the Puritan community of Salem, who cannot believe his forebears were anything but
pure of heart (Hawthorne, 89, 1987). Hawthorne was excavating his
own family history as his great-great-great grandfather John
Hathorne had been a judge in the Salem Witch Trials (Dobie, 31,
2012). The protagonist Brown in the story is brought to a moral
reckoning with the behavior of those closest to him – his religious
teachers, political leaders, and his wife – poignantly named Faith by
Hawthorne. Ultimately, Brown cannot come to terms with the reality of his kin's sinful past, let alone his own – and Hawthorne seems
to doubt the reader can as well. "Had Goodman Brown fallen asleep
in the forest and dreamed a wild dream of a witch meeting?" Hawthorne muses near the story's close. "Be it so if you will; but alas, it
was a dream of evil omen for young Goodman Brown" (Hawthorne,

100). Hawthorne's cynicism ("Be it so if you will") is directed as much to his readers as to the history of the New England founding. In short, Hawthorne's is perhaps the first work in American fiction directly attempting to revise the false narrative of a "pure" and guiltless founding.

A writer with a level of penetrating understanding of human nature and American society such as Hawthorne's could only show an allegory for the willful erasures of history – and hope for the best. It is no small wonder, then, that another writer of similar gothic understandings of American life – Shirley Jackson – would present the central victim of her greatest American horror story as a housewife named Hutchinson. Taken in its broadest sociopolitical context, "The Lottery" belongs in the realm of dialogue with Puritan history as much as it does in its prescient feel for disquietude found in mid-twentieth-century American domesticity and the undercurrent of violence present therein. Indeed, while the story's shocking ending leaves the darkest of lasting impressions, it's the details of Jackson's new-fashioned New England village that haunt – the dishes in the sink, the faded dresses of the wives, and the white-shirted men in blue jeans. This is Salem transplanted to the twentieth century – a world where "the girls stood aside" (Jackson, 210, 2005). Hawthorne and Jackson in their own ways capture the continuity of the uniformity of Puritan thought over the centuries – and how it mattered for their times; Hawthorne's was marked by Indian removal and genocide, while Jackson's was characterized by the Holocaust and the terrors of racial oppression.

"The Americans form at once a Puritan nation and a commercial people," Tocqueville wrote (Tocqueville, 565). "[T]heir religious beliefs as well as their industrial habits therefore bring them to exact from woman a self-abnegation and a continual sacrifice of her pleasures to her business that is rare to demand of her in Europe" (Tocqueville, 565). Both Church and joint-stock companies were instrumental in laying down the contradictory American ethos of acquisitiveness and restraint. Women – more specifically, white women – were at once afforded greater privileges in America based on the need to establish permanent settlements. They were therefore encouraged to become part of the colonial enterprise while limiting their sexual agency, lest other blood taint Englishness. Women's domestic labor was at the fore of the colonial enterprise – it created the kind of freedom to exploit the land and its resources not quite possible in the same way in Spanish America. It is no accident that much of Jackson's story "The Lottery" is replete with allusions to work. In fact, the theme surrounds the savage business at hand. The pressing concern is for it to be over, so folks can "get back to work" (Jackson, 295).

The need for labor in the colonies produced any number of paradoxes and contradictory practices. The importation of Africans to make up for labor shortages had a somewhat liberating effect on white women, some of whom were freed from the task of breastfeeding through the use of black wet nurses, especially in the South (Treckel, 47, 1996). American political thought learned to countenance at once the intimate relationship with Africans while erecting social and political barriers to the presumption of their equality with whites. This path was not linear, and the development of a consciously racialized legal and religious rationale for black inferiority and subjectivity began to emerge by the mid-seventeenth century. The ways in which this system – foremost a system of thought – was fashioned cannot be understood outside the context of efforts to establish English hegemony across the Atlantic, an effort demanding careful attention to proscribing the humanity of indigenous and black populations – while regulating the related role and status of white women.

The African Presence in the English Colonies

The Trinidadian historian Eric Williams' classic work *Capitalism and Slavery* made an important but often overlooked point about slavery. "Slavery was not born of racism," he wrote. "[R]ather, racism was the consequence of slavery" (Williams, 7, 1994). Given that historically slave labor involved "brown, white, black, and yellow; Catholic, Protestant, and pagan," Williams explored the material basis behind the so-called peculiar institution (Williams, 7). This emphasis did not lack for subtlety, as Williams likewise noted that slavery's economic bases in the Americas had theoretical antecedents in European political thought, especially that of Adam Smith. "White servitude," Williams wrote, "was the historic base upon which Negro slavery was constructed" (Williams, 19). Recent works in political history underscore this point, but it was an unusual if not astounding proposition when Williams made it in the mid-1940s.

American political thought became intensely racialized early on, and very much linked to this transition from white to black free labor. As

Ralph Ellison noted in his allegorical chapter on the history of racism in America (camouflaged in the scene where his protagonist learns the science behind the making of white paint), whiteness' association with freedom became part of the economic engine of America:

> "You know the best selling paint we got, the one that *made* this here business?" he asked as I helped him fill a vat with a smelly substance.
> "No, I don't."
> "Our white, Optic White."
> "Why the white rather than the others?"
> "'Cause we started stressing it from the first."
> (Ellison, 217, 1995)

America's early colonial emphasis on whiteness arose out of failed efforts to incorporate white servitude, and later Indian slavery, effectively. Africans became the "solution" to labor needs – particularly in the southern colonies – making the path to a color-based system of slavery the sine qua non for economic growth. As Ellison expressed it, it was whiteness "that made this here business." Edmund S. Morgan placed the year when "it became more advantageous for Virginians to buy slaves" rather than employ indentured servants at 1660 (Morgan, 299, 1975). Those slaves bought were Africans; their color soon became associated with moral and intellectual inferiority. English religious thought took a turn as well. "Before the 1660s," Morgan noted, "it seems to have been assumed that Christianity and slavery were incompatible" (Morgan, 331). That changed to suit Virginia planters' economic interests and the social challenges of racially unified uprisings – best exemplified by Bacon's Rebellion in 1676. Whether Morgan's pivotal year of 1660 is unquestionable is beside the point; at some indeterminate moment in the last quarter of the seventeenth century, changing customs in the Virginia Commonwealth made faith, capital, and race interlocking parts of a civically exclusionary political thought. Bacon's Rebellion – a multiracial uprising – forced a pivotal redirection of the Virginian propertied class' understanding of labor as necessarily marked by racial divisions.

Finally, the status of white women was changed during this process. "It was in the area of sexual relations that the authorities were most assiduous to separate the races," Morgan wrote (Morgan, 333). Unlike the Spanish and French, who countenanced a racial pigmentocracy premised upon acceptance of interracial intimacy, the English did not. This would become a defining component of many American legislatures, as Randall Kennedy noted. "Between the 1660s and 1960s, forty-one colonies or states enacted racial laws regulating sex or marriage" (Kennedy, 18, 2003). Kennedy's study was keen to point out that despite the stigmatization of many other ethnic groups of color, blacks occupied the group excluded from racial intimacy in every instance historically (Kennedy, 18). The threat to white "impurity" or "degeneration" thus became linked with a limited but peculiarly exalted status of white women in American society. It was an ideal associated with civic inferiority, a protected social status, and economic stability. The ideal was frequently unmet, but it retained its appeal in literature well into the twentieth century. When Tom Buchanan rails against the ills of modernity in *The Great Gatsby*, we get an incredulous reply from Jordan Baker:

> Nowadays people begin by sneering at family life, and family institutions, and next they'll throw everything overboard and have intermarriage between black and white. Flushed with his impassioned gibberish, he [Tom] saw himself standing alone on the last barrier of civilization.
> "We're all white here," murmured Jordan.
>
> (Fitzgerald, 130)

Of course, for Tom, the absence of nonwhites in his privileged circle was insufficient to assuage his fear of what was happening "out there" to the broader white world that might be collapsing around him.

Despite Tocqueville's close association with slavery and the Virginian founding, New England was as influential in cultivating a theology of racial inferiority that buoyed slavery and the subordination of blacks in America. Ibram X. Kendi's book *Stamped from the Beginning: The Definitive History of Racist Ideas in America* addresses the absence of such critical inquiry in Puritan political thought in New England. As Kendi points out, it was Cotton Mather who argued in his *A Good Master Well Served* (1696) that Africans were "[B]etter fed and clothed, & better managed by far, than you would be, if you were your own men" (Kendi, 63). The type of historical "forgetting" alluded to by Ernest Renan is worth revisiting here, as Kendi describes it:

> Mather's writings on slavery spread throughout the colonies, influencing enslavers from Boston to Virginia. By the eighteenth century, he had published more books than any other American, and his native Boston had become colonial America's booming intellectual center. Boston was now on the periphery of a booming slave society centered in the tidewater region of Maryland, Virginia, and northeastern Carolina.
>
> (Kendi, 64)

Mather's theology set a racial standard for Christian equality, making white souls the object for emulation (Kendi, 59). Such teachings launched a racialist vision of American life, one in which color became an essential feature for marking out the character of human beings.

Racial formation in America moved from religious premises to scientific arguments by the eighteenth century (Omi and Winant, 63, 1994). The Enlightenment sought "rational" bases for the establishment of white supremacy, making claims that were different from those in the early colonial period. Tocqueville remarked upon this transition, arguing that where "Christianity had destroyed servitude; Christians of the sixteenth century reestablished it; they nevertheless accepted it only as an exception in their social system and they took care to restrict it to a single one of the human races," as he wrote in *Democracy in America* (Tocqueville, 326–327). The newly racialized nature of slavery made black life tinged with the mark of inferiority. "You can make the Negro free," Tocqueville observed, "but you cannot do it so that he is not in the position of a stranger vis-à-vis the European" (Tocqueville, 327). Thus, even in freedom, the American social and political system marginalized African Americans, whose very color became "the external sign of [their] ignominy" (Tocqueville, 327).

Wilson Carey McWilliams' classic work *The Idea of Fraternity in America* grasped the shift from early American racism to that of its scientific offspring. "The idea of a 'fraternity' particular to members of a given 'race' sat badly with traditional Christianity," he wrote, what with all humans deriving from Adam (McWilliams, 174, 1973). "Since Enlightenment thought tended to begin with the premise of 'original equality,' it had little affinity with racism," McWilliams noted. Yet the Enlightenment "also affirmed the right of property and the legitimacy of interest so strongly as to blunt any opposition to the existing institution" (McWilliams, 175). The connection to capital and the rights of the "individual" was sufficient grounds to justify slavery, where monogenesis (a single creation through Adam and Eve) made the argument more difficult. In time, polygenetic origins crowded into American Christian teachings, along with a theology of degenerative origins, most notably that of the "Sons of Ham."

In the end, eighteenth-century political thought in America was less tied to religious teaching; empiricism and reason were to govern human affairs. The radicalism of the American Revolution was about a break from not only English political tutelage, but also from traditional, pre-scientific thought. Ironically, this thought – shaped by the material, cultural, and social exchanges rooted in conflict between Europeans and the nonwhite societies they encountered – developed exquisite hypotheses as to the superiority of whites, giving the concept of race life, and the reality of physical differences among humans a deterministic quality. That these factors were shaped uniquely in an American context where liberalism and the ideas of political liberty were being reconsidered outside the limits of European economic and geographical realities made the American experience indeed exceptional, if not for the reasons and ends often coincident with that term.

American Political Thought to the French and Indian War

Readers of *The Great Gatsby* discover F. Scott Fitzgerald's novel contains an ode to the eighteenth century's most famous, and perhaps most influential, American, Benjamin Franklin. Near the end of the story, after Gatsby's death, we learn of Jay Gatz's personal schedule – what we'd today call a "daily plan" (Fitzgerald, 173). In it, we see it bears a striking resemblance to that of Franklin's: the words *rise, wash* [*bath*], *work, read, study, resolve* [*resolutions*] appear in both texts. Gatsby's schedule contains a clear nod to Franklin at the outset – "study electricity" – and it is evident Fitzgerald wants to remind us that the best and worst of what Gatsby represents go back to Franklin and the earliest of modern American political thought (Franklin, 88, 1986).

As a self-professed "self-made" man, Franklin became the archetype of what it means to be an American – namely an *individual*. This liberal vision of personal discipline in the acquisition of wealth marked a turning point in colonial values, moving from more community-based forms of identity to something approaching Ralph Waldo Emerson's ideal of an unattached, freethinking person. Where family and faith had previously guided American thought, Wilson Carey McWilliams explained the transition best embodied by Franklin's ethos as one where "Science and acquisition would lead man to a state of plenty which would remove the shortcomings of the 'state of nature'" (McWilliams, 183). Franklin's *The Way to Wealth* (1758) and *The Art of Virtue* (1784) were the earliest and best in a long line of American self-help books, a concept whose descriptive title strains our common understanding of what "help" actually is – namely an act necessitating the assistance of others.

It was John Wise who argued in his *Vindication of the Government of Churches* in 1717 that "every Man must be conceived to be perfectly in his own Power and disposal, and not to be controuled by the Authority of any other" – thus affirming an individual's right to consent to be ruled by the government (Kramnick and Lowi, 35, 2009). The influence of the Enlightenment on colonial churches and assemblies grew over the century, and American leaders began to assert a new ideology of rights while limiting those of nonwhites and women. As James P. Young writes, "What Locke's view of the human nature of man offered, for all its ambiguity, was the possibility of developing a rationally based theory for the protection of human rights"; and yet those protections were not afforded to Africans, whose enslavement Locke would later profit from as a member of the Royal African Company (Young, 27, 1996). The liberal creed that became identified with America was from its inception deeply skeptical, if not outright antagonistic towards the rights and basic humanity of blacks. As Robert Bernasconi and Anika Maaza Mann put it, Locke helped establish the norms by which a racialized form of American slavery came into being (Bernasconi and Mann, 90, 2005).

When rights were commonly spoken of in eighteenth-century America, they were usually in reference to those of Englishmen. As Walter McDougall notes in his *A New American History, 1585–1828*, white conceptions of liberty varied among "four sorts of Britons and Germans." These conceptions nevertheless constituted a form of unity through the practice of slavery:

> [T]he very existence and scale of the institution of slavery forced colonists of European stock to make such tortuous adjustments in their notions of liberty and justice that one might argue the colonies (especially in the south) were Africanized as much as slaves were Americanized.
>
> (McDougall, 155)

As Gordon Wood explained the changing dynamics in nineteenth century America, "Powerful social and economic developments were stretching, fraying, and forcing apart older personal bonds holding people together, and people everywhere were hard pressed to explain what was happening" (Wood, 11, 1992). Despite the fact that traditional mores remained largely intact, they were under assault. Religious diversity and deistic philosophy marked one type of challenge; others included the growing presence of Africans, and poor white laborers – indentured servants whose ethnic makeup at times was pit against Anglo-American racial ideals. Finally, the changing nature of commercial relations and the slow but steady movement towards institutions of capital, primitive though they were, made local economic relationships less certain than they had been. The new American political thought of liberal economics and emergent political republicanism did not truly advance until the last quarter of the century, but the shape of things to come could be discerned by the Seven Years' War at mid-century. "The English thought they lived in a republicanized monarchy, and they were right," Wood wrote in his *The Radicalism of the American Revolution* (Wood, 98). This meant the acceptance of British monarchy, along with the attendant rights of British subjects. As the retention of these rights was called into question, so too was the authority of British rule.

The conclusion of the French and Indian War created the political and geographical imperatives for challenging British rule over the colonies. Seeing themselves as no longer formally hemmed in by the French presence in America, British colonial subjects in America had a heightened sense of their rights in the aftermath of a bloody conflict centered on territorial claims in the Ohio Valley. They were mistaken, as "King George proclaimed a vast 'Indian Preserve' between the Appalachians and Mississippi River, effectively hemming in his American colonists along the Atlantic coast just as the French had done previously" (Borneman, xxiii, 2006).

But agitation against England was largely divided along generational lines, with older political leaders such as George Washington, John Dickinson, and John Adams more reticent to strain ties with the mother country (Rakove, 15, 2010). Radicalization towards revolution came as much in the practice of the act, if not in its conception, as Hannah Arendt later proffered (Rakove, 18).

Beyond the political implications of the war between Britain and France, the meaning of national identity was memorialized in the aftermath of the conflict. Cooper's novel *The Last of the Mohicans*, written during the period of Jacksonian westward expansion, reflected upon the war as a moment of racial imprinting upon the nation. As M.R. Song has written:

> Although the war between Britain and France works as the setting of the story, the conflict between the white and the native is more prominent. The geographical location is the frontier of the North America, the border between the white and the Indian. No matter who would succeed the war of these two countries, the white group is the winner, for the native tribes are gradually colonized. In this way, the white expand the boundary slowly. Actually, expanding the boundary and conquering the uncivilized Indian are an essential aspect of a national identity. The colonization of the white on the land is moralized and the domination of the white is authorized.
>
> (Song, 32, 2016)

White liberty and expansionism thus became critical components of the formation of historical memory, first in the colonies, and later in the newly independent country. That this memorialization endured a shift from a form of conservative republicanism (monarchy) to that of a revolutionary stripe (independence) should not negate its underlying significance in creating "American" identity.

Conclusion

By 1763, British colonists in America began asserting their rights as subjects more forcefully, albeit still largely within the context of those bearing loyalty to the monarchy. This conservatism of subjects (and citizens) carrying obligations was, and is, at the heart of American republicanism, a philosophy very much opposed to revolution. Even the acceptability of America's revolution would be constricted in time to that of a radical but limited departure from adherence to the law and custom. Enlightenment thought – particularly that of Locke – elevated the possibility and virtue of revolution; but it did not extend it to general governance or to racial minorities or women. This conservatism towards revolution and what would later be called "social engineering" gave America the bearings of a progressive nation while steeping it in more traditional, if not reactionary, politics. The conundrum was best captured in a 1973 interview between the conservative journalist and icon William F. Buckley, Jr. and the Black Panther Party's self-avowed revolutionary leader Huey P. Newton, who asked Buckley a simple yet profound question:

Mr. Newton: I have a friend who's almost dying for me to ask this question, if you will. The question is, during the Revolution of 1776, when the United States broke away from England, my friend would like to know which side you would have been on at that time?

Mr. Buckley: I think probably ... would have been on the side of George Washington. I'm not absolutely sure because it remains to be established historically whether what we sought to prove at that point might not have been proved by more peaceful means. On the whole, I'm against revolutions, though I think as revolutions go, that was a pretty humane one.

Mr. Newton: Yes, you're not such a bad guy after all. My friend will be surprised to hear that, I hope he's listening.[2]

Buckley's Paradox – conservatism's acceptance of America's revolutionary origins – must be tied to American exceptionalism. If America's revolutionary experience in the world is unique because it gave birth to a nation by which all other revolutions outside the republican mode become unnecessary, then radical national origins can be accepted. The eighteenth-century movement from traditional, religious-based values of truth, rooted in local experience, gave way to a broad, universal liberalism – at least for whites – one that made claims beyond faith, station, and locale. That this tension was abated somewhat by denying the universalist claims to women and nonwhites does not erase all of its significance. But it does help to explain its peculiar genesis. In this light, the American political thought of the revolutionary period has great explanatory power for the nation that would emerge.

Notes

1. www.congress.gov/resources/display/content/The+Federalist+Papers#TheFederalist Papers-1.
2. www.oac.cdlib.org/findaid/ark:/13030/kt6m3nc88c/dsc/#c01-1.2.11.1.

References

Valerie Babb, *Whiteness Visible: The Meaning of Whiteness in American Literature and Culture* (New York: New York University Press, 1998).

Robert Bernasconi and Anika Maaza Mann, *The Contradictions of Racism: Locke, Slavery, and the Two Treatises* (Ithaca, NY: Cornell University Press, 2005).

Walter R. Borneman, *The French and Indian War: Deciding the Fate of North America* (New York: HarperCollins, 2006).

James W. Ceaser, *Designing a Polity: America's Constitution in Theory and Practice* (Lanham, MD: Rowan and Littlefield, 2011).

William Cronon, *Changes in the Land: Indians, Colonists, and the Ecology of New England* (New York: Hill and Wang, 2003).

Ann B. Dobie, *Theory into Practice: An Introduction to Literary Criticism* (Boston, MA: Wadsworth, 2012).

W.E.B. Du Bois, *The Souls of Black Folks* (New York: W.W. Norton, 1999).

Roxanne Dunbar-Ortiz, *An Indigenous People's History of the United States* (Boston, MA: Beacon Press, 2014).

Ralph Ellison, *Invisible Man* (New York: Vintage, 1995).

F. Scott Fitzgerald, *The Great Gatsby* (New York: Scribner, 2004).

Benjamin Franklin, *The Autobiography and Other Writings* (New York: Penguin Books, 1986).

Alexander Hamilton, John Jay, and James Madison, *The Federalist* (New York: J. & A. McLean, 1788).

Nathaniel Hawthorne, *Young Goodman Brown and Other Tales* (Brian Harding, Ed.) (Oxford, UK: Oxford University Press, 1987).

Audrey Horning, *Ireland in the Virginia Sea: Colonialism in the British Atlantic* (Chapel Hill, NC: Omohundro Institute and University of North Carolina Press, 2017).

Shirley Jackson, *The Lottery and Other Stories* (New York: Farrar, Straus, and Giroux, 2005).

Ibram X. Kendi, *Stamped from the Beginning: The Definitive History of Racist Ideas in America* (New York: Nation Books, 2016).

Randall Kennedy, *Interracial Intimacies: Sex, Marriage, Identity, and Adoption* (New York: First Vintage Books, 2003).

Isaac Kramnick and Theodore Lowi, *American Political Thought* (New York: W.W. Norton, 2009).

Jill Lepore, *The Name of War: King Philip's War and the Origins of American Identity* (New York: Vintage Books, 1999).

Charles Mann, *1491: New Revelations of the Americas before Columbus* (New York: Vintage, 2011).

Walter A. McDougall, *Freedom Just around the Corner: A New American History, 1585–1828* (New York: HarperCollins, 2004).

Wilson Carey McWilliams, *The Idea of Fraternity in America* (Berkeley, CA: University of California Press, 1973).

Edmunds S. Morgan, *American Slavery, American Freedom* (New York: W.W. Norton, 1975).

James A. Morone, *Hellfire Nation: The Politics of Sin in American History* (New Haven, CT: Yale University Press, 2003).

Michael Omi and Howard Winant, *Racial Formation in the United States: From the 1960s to the 1990s* (New York: Routledge, 1994).

Jack Rakove, *Revolutionaries: A New History of the Invention of America* (New York: Houghton Mifflin, 2010).

Ernest Renan, *What Is a Nation? And Other Political Writings* (New York: Columbia University Press, 2018).

Rogers Smith, *Civic Ideals: Conflicting Visions of Citizenship in US History* (New Haven, CT: Yale University Press, 1997).

M.R. Song, "The Othered Indian: Cultural Appropriation, and Formation of National Identity in *The Last of the Mohicans*," *Cross-Cultural Communication*, 12(7), 28–33, 2016.

Alexis de Tocqueville, *Democracy in America* (Harvey Mansfield and Delba Winthrop, Eds.) (Chicago, IL: University of Chicago Press, 2000).

Paula A. Treckel, *To Comfort the Heart: Women in Seventeenth-Century America* (New York: Twayne, 1996).

Keith Whittington, *American Political Thought: Readings and Materials* (Oxford, UK: Oxford University Press, 2017).

Eric Williams, *Capitalism and Slavery* (Chapel Hill, NC: University of North Carolina Press, 1994).

Garry Wills, *Lincoln at Gettysburg: The Words that Remade a Nation* (New York: Simon and Schuster, 1992).

Gordon S. Wood, *The Radicalism of the American Revolution* (New York: Alfred A. Knopf, 1992).

James P. Young, *Reconsidering American Liberalism: The Troubled Odyssey of the Liberal Idea* (Boulder, CO: Westview Press, 1996).

Chapter Two
Revolution and Order: 1763–1800

Introduction

Before considering whether or not the American Revolution was radical, it is worth asking why that question matters a great deal to historians and political theorists. When the historian Ira Katznelson recently wanted to explain the magnitude and importance of the New Deal to American history, he compared it to the French Revolution, not the American, giving it "an import almost on par with the French Revolution" (Katznelson, 9, 2013). On the other hand, Gordon Wood's work on the American Revolution put radicalism at the fore, suggesting that *The Radicalism of the American Revolution*, as both title and historical fact, was a reality beyond the understanding of most Americans when considering the origins of their country (Wood, 1992). The unstated point is that nobody needs to write about the "radicalism" of the French, Russian, or Chinese revolutions, to cite the most obvious comparisons. Everyone understands those events were radical by any measure. Perhaps Hannah Arendt overstated it when she declared, "The sad truth of the matter is that the French Revolution, which ended in disaster, has made world history, while the American Revolution, so triumphantly successful, has remained an event of little more than local importance" (Arendt, 45, 2006).

Yet Arendt was a great admirer of the American Revolution. And despite most historians' aversion to drawing radical conclusions about it, the American Revolution's significance is hard to overstate. It was the first republican revolution in modern times, limited though it was. But why the debate over its degree of profundity? One reason has to do with the nature of change brought about by the American Revolution, and the inevitable comparisons with those that came after it – including the often overlooked Haitian Revolution, which gave modern republicanism its first claim to a liberty unencumbered by attachment to slavery.

John Adams famously asked "But what do we mean by the American Revolution?" in his 1818 letter to H. Niles, some 35 years after the Peace of Paris officially ended the conflict. His response was that at its heart the radical change that brought about the Revolution was "in the principles, opinions, sentiments, and affections of the people." This was "the real American revolution."[1] This shift in sentiments was about the meaning of Englishness, the legitimacy of Great Britain's authority over the colonies, and the obligations of subjects to the crown. In this light, at least for Adams, the Revolution was largely an act of political severance; it was Thomas Jefferson's Declaration of Independence that contained the seeds of complete human freedom. It is the tension between Adams's reflection and Jeffersonian projection that make the American Revolution's standing within American political thought uneven and hard to nail down. Part of the political genius of Abraham Lincoln was that he provided, perhaps more than any person (certainly any elected political figure), depth of meaning to both the Revolution and Jefferson's words in the Declaration.

What follows, then, is necessarily a debate of sorts over forms of republicanism limited to principles tied very closely to white racial democracy produced during the Enlightenment. Indeed, many of the revolutionary principles of the eighteenth century were those developed in hindsight – a look back at Rome and other historic republics – rather than to a future of unbridled representative government without respect to race. There are flashes of that thought in Jefferson, though they are joined by other less farsighted conclusions. Indeed, by pressing for order over a revolutionary national ethos, the Framers of the Constitution also further entrenched white supremacy and patriarchy into the national story.

Riding to Philadelphia

History has not recorded what, if anything, Thomas Jefferson and Robert Hemings spoke about during their weeklong journey from Jefferson's Monticello home in Virginia to Philadelphia in May of 1776. Hemings was 14, while Jefferson was 33. Jefferson owned Hemings as his slave, and would later father children through Hemings' sister Sally, aged three at the time of the journey, which was entirely on horseback. No one else accompanied the two. Hemings served as Jefferson's body servant in Philadelphia during the weeks leading up to the signing of the Declaration of Independence. He seems to have provided Jefferson's meals, his tea, and oil to light his lamps. The two men occupied quarters on Seventh and Market Streets beginning on May 23 in Philadelphia. The house was owned by the bricklayer Jacob Graff. Hemings likely slept in the attic or garret of Graff's home for the duration of their stay (Ellis, 2015).

In 1776 Jefferson undertook a personal census of his household; it included some 83 slaves. But there is something beyond the numbers that is illuminated in Jefferson and Hemings' ride to Philadelphia – something that speaks not only to Jefferson's and the nation's history of slavery, but to the ways in which political thought is often sanitized. Here were two people – one a boy, the other one of the nation's leading political thinkers – sharing space so intimately over the course of several months. And yet that space has been recorded as part of a single line of action – America's movement towards Independence. It has not been presented widely as part of the dynamic of white Herrenvolk or racialized democracy.

The irony of Jefferson's ownership of Hemings extends to the historic commemoration of black and indigenous peoples in the nation's history as set pieces – or worse, as invisible. This was the warning given by Ernest Renan, alluded to at the beginning of Chapter One. Bob Hemings and his boyhood ride with Jefferson to Philadelphia in 1776 is an object lesson in how the documentation of American political thought is at times more concerned with documents than the silences that no physical document can query – and yet are no less lacking in importance. Even the best works in American political thought are more likely to make note of the fact that Jefferson's original draft of the Declaration included a provision objecting to King George III's waging of "cruel war against human nature itself" through slavery, while neglecting to mention that Jefferson himself owned dozens of slaves at the time.

Jefferson's draft of the Declaration was edited in committee, a fact that pained him a great deal. Yet, despite the attention given to the Committee's removal of his anti-slavery language, less attention has been paid to language left in the final draft related to Native Americans. One of the many charges Jefferson leveled against the British King was that "He has excited domestic insurrections amongst us, and has endeavored to bring on the inhabitants of our frontiers, the merciless Indian Savages, whose known rule of warfare, is an undistinguished destruction of all ages, sexes and conditions" (Kramnick and Lowi, 154, 2009). Thus, a twofold principle of American political order was established at the outset. The first was frontier insecurity and the perceived need to conquer to uphold civilization. This would later morph into prioritizing the maintenance of a rules-based global system by force – what one historian would allude to as the "Roman predicament" America had gotten itself into (James, 2008). The second principle was an anti-indigenous disposition justifying expansion and removal. Jefferson was thus instrumental in laying the foundation of these twin notions of American liberty – and he was president at the inception of its implementation with the Louisiana Purchase, a subject covered in Chapter Three.

And yet Huey P. Newton's Black Panther Party platform, created in 1966, cited the entirety of Jefferson's opening lines to the Declaration of Independence, word for word (Carpini, 2000). As evidenced in his interview with William F. Buckley mentioned at the close of Chapter One, Newton and the Panthers (and numerous anti-colonial movements around the world) recognized the American Revolution's radicalism in its advocacy of upending those governments that opposed the interests and rights of their people. Gordon Wood's assessment that the type of equality envisioned by Jefferson was radical insofar as it presumed "everyone was really the same as everyone else" without specifying some specific equality of opportunity or outcome is notable (Wood, 234). Human equality was a condition of birth – inequality presumably was a condition of what one did thereafter. Of course, Jefferson's radicalism extended to recognizing that social and economic inequalities were often the byproduct of history – what we'd refer to today as structural inequalities; this was especially true after his time in France. While Jefferson's republican vision did not transform the nature of American slavery (it in fact further entrenched it, as I will discuss in Chapter Three), his intellectual honesty on the subject did evince numerous rejections of the institution – if only for posterity (Matthews, 66–67, 1984).

When Alex Haley's iconic novel *Roots* was released in January of 1977 on American television, one of its effects was to pour cold water on the yearlong celebrations associated with the American bicentennial. Haley's brief allusion to how the enslaved were notified about the Declaration of Independence was powerful, if pithy: "They heard next that another Continental Congress had met, with a group of massas from Virginia moving for complete separation from the English" (Haley, 359, 1974). That "group of massas from Virginia" and their northern compatriots did in fact heavily influence America's push for liberty. But they could not rescue the idea of liberty from its racially charged premises. Abraham Lincoln understood this in 1864 when he addressed a crowd in Baltimore, then the heart of the critical slave-holding state of Maryland:

> The world has never had a good definition of the word liberty, and the American people, just now, are much in want of one. We all declare for liberty, but in using the same word, we do not all mean the same thing. With some the word liberty may mean for each man to do as he pleases with himself, and the product of his labor; while with others the same word may mean for some men to do as they please with other men, and the product of other men's labor.
>
> (Burlingame, 33, 1994)

Alexis de Tocqueville's view that American democracy was in large measure a radical enterprise based on the social equality of its citizens contained an analytical half-truth commensurate with the limited nature of American liberty – a liberty that included the right to enslave, separate, rape, sell, and brutalize millions of members of society. Equality was protected by uneven distributions of citizenship, property, and social rights among whites. As Rogers Smith has written:

> The universalist, egalitarian claims of inalienable rights with which the Declaration began rested uncomfortably with the denunciation of Indian "savages" and the silence on women and African American slavery that followed however smoothly the rhetoric flowed for those who regarded racial and gender hierarchies as natural.
>
> (Smith, 81, 1997)

Forging a new government in both theory and practice upon such a premise would only entrench the hollow liberty alluded to by Lincoln decades later.

Articles of Confederation

While Alexis de Tocqueville fails to mention the Declaration of Independence in *Democracy in America*, it is notable, if not equally astounding, that he makes one spare mention of the Articles of Confederation. It is a passing reference, and a criticism at that: "[A]lthough the laws that constituted this union [1777–1787] were defective, the common bond subsisted despite them" (Tocqueville, 105). Tocqueville's occlusion of the Articles from consideration in his study presaged later political scientists' and historians' less than kind view of them. American high school students are drilled in its deficiencies: failure to raise revenues from the individual states, no coercive executive power to speak of, failure to create a single currency – and on it goes. But the Articles had its defenders, and in some respects its Anti-Federalist brand of republicanism illustrates the strident turn towards empire some would see in the creation of the American Constitution – while likewise revealing different deficiencies of its own.

Few contemporary political theorists – certainly in the last 40 years – have been as ebullient about the Articles, and more importantly, the brand of republicanism espoused by its adherents, than the late Wilson Carey McWilliams. While McWilliams never went as far as Theodore Lowi in suggesting that the Constitutional Convention was a coup by another name (Lowi, 2009), he did see it as a departure from the politics of virtue to the politics of order (McWilliams, 183, 2011). Under the Articles of Confederation, smaller, more intimate republics were made possible, with civic virtue and traditional (read as religious) mores looked upon as the bedrock of the public good. In McWilliams' words, the Framers of the Constitution "believed in natural rights and in an idea of freedom that emphasizes the individual's private capacities, treating the public good, for the most part, as an aggregate of private interests" (McWilliams, 184).

Speaking of coups, James P. Young has written that given that "the convention procedures ignored the fact that the delegates were authorized only to amend, not to produce an entirely new constitution," the result was "an example of a form of counterrevolutionary coup d'état" (Young, 57, 1996). For theorists like McWilliams and Young, supportive of the civic republican ideal that is most associated with the small government structures that preceded the Constitution, the coup was as much ideological as it was procedural. The challenge with the Jeffersonian ward-republic view of American self-government before the Constitution, however, is that it seldom evaluates its commitment to chattel slavery and white supremacy. The great exception was the passage of the Northwest Ordinance, which banned slavery in the acquired territories (although it supported the return of fugitive slaves) (Smith, 99). A key caveat was that its limited application to the northwest strongly implied slavery would not be excluded from new territories and states south of the Ohio River (McDougall, 289, 2004). A similarly repressive stance was taken against the rights and interests of Native Americans and women under the Articles as well (Smith, 108–114). Only the viability of Indian resistance made their status within the political system ambiguous (Smith, 107).

As early as 1780, Alexander Hamilton was writing that "the fundamental defects" in the Articles, "is a want of power in Congress" (Kramnick and Lowi, 162). He had concluded in his letter to James Duane that the "Confederation itself is defective, and requires to be altered. It is neither fit for war, nor peace" (Kramnick and Lowi, 164). The Articles lacked the power necessary for the type of government – or more precisely, the type of nation – Hamilton envisioned America becoming. The vision of a strong, commercial republic with expansionist interests was already present. Madison came to the same conclusion, but for different reasons. His interest was in a functional government able to execute its laws within a three-branch political system (Rakove, 364–365, 2010). He was less preoccupied with the type of "energy" in government in the form of a chief executive than Hamilton, but nevertheless saw a need for such a figure.

The decision to reconsider republican forms while holding to republican principles was part of the theoretical heavy lifting the Framers of the Constitution had to undertake. The success of the Revolution imposed a paradox, however: a nation formed under the radical banner of the right to "alter or abolish" its government was now turning towards the virtue of order and stability *in* government. Americans today know of whom they speak when they invoke the term "Founding Fathers," a phrase first popularized by President Warren G. Harding in 1916. They are not speaking of those who drafted and signed the Articles of Confederation as such. And it is to the Constitution that Alexis de Tocqueville went to draw upon the strengths of the American political system. The relative invisibility of the Articles in political discourse is at once understandable, but also suggestive. It speaks to a turn towards not only a different structural form of government, but also, perhaps, one in principle – and for some – one with distinctive normative tradeoffs.

The Political Thought of the American Constitution

A republic, if you can keep it.

Shays' Rebellion has long been seen as the precipitating event for convening the Constitutional Convention (Rakove, 33–34). A similarly chaotic uprising – one brought about by New York doctors whose robbery of the city's cemeteries for fresh bodies for medical research led to riots – is said to have brought about the call for a strong New York governorship that became the model for the national executive (Thach, 2010). Whatever historical marker one finds more explanatory than another, the Articles of Confederation was seen as lacking the kind of force necessary for keeping a republic. Those who convened first in Annapolis and later in Philadelphia were looking for political stability – a point of focus for the next half-century. Indeed, Lincoln's reflections at Gettysburg were deeply motivated by the prospect that self-government might well not "long endure." As Paul Frymer has written:

> After a tumultuous first few years following independence, national leaders quickly coalesced around the argument that a stronger central government was essential in order for the nation to expand its territory safely and securely over this land contested by Native Americans, European colonists, restless settlers, economic entrepreneurs, and ambitious state legislators.
>
> (Frymer, 34, 2017)

The implicit challenge was the question of centralization itself. Patrick Henry's famous oration opposed to the new constitution delivered at the Virginia Ratifying Convention in June of 1788 was keen on the point of the states yielding local authority to new, centralized institutions – particularly the new president. "Some way or other we must be a great and mighty empire," he said. "[W]e must have an army, and a navy, and a number of things. When the American spirit was in its youth, the language of America was different; liberty, sir, was then the primary object" (Kramnick and Lowi, 272).

Henry's eloquence lost the day, however. Moreover, his and the majority of the Anti-Federalists' interpretations of liberty countenanced chattel slavery. As Lincoln suggested, "liberty" lacked a common understanding in American politics. But the same may also be said generally about the Constitution. The historian Jack Rakove has reminded us that perhaps the best the Framers could provide were "meanings" – in plural – rather than any singular "original meaning" to the Constitution (Rakove, 2010). American conservatives have tended to view the idea of a living understanding of the Constitution as mistaken, if not subversive to liberty. American liberals have tended to view multiple understandings of the Constitution as a source of national strength, if not the ultimate form of patriotism. It is worth noting that the American Constitution produced in its time a secondary document, nearly as revered by many, for defending it.

The *Federalist Papers* occupy a unique place in the history of republicanism insofar as they preemptively rebuked attacks on the new political order before it came into being. James P. Young summarized this point well:

> If as [the political theorist] Sheldon Wolin rightly argues, only the text but not the meaning of the Constitution had been agreed upon then the place of The Federalist as the first systematic attempt to elucidate the elusive "intent of the Framers" made it almost uniquely important. Whether or not they captured the intent (or even whether there was a single determinate intent), the papers have been treated as if they did, and it is that perception that has left a deep impression on constitutional theory and development.
>
> (Young, 58)

But not long after the Constitution was ratified, those who drafted *The Federalist* were at odds over basic features of the document. By 1793,

James Madison's belief that his earliest fears that "legislative encroach-ments" would disrupt the delicate system of checks and balances of the Constitution had shifted to those emanating from the executive branch (Rakove, 364). It was in this year that Madison and Alexander Hamil-ton took to writing about the Constitution again – only this time as adversaries – in their written debates over the Proclamation of Neutral-ity. Where Hamilton saw a clearly defined right of the president to proclaim a state of neutrality for the United States with respect to the conflicts engulfing Europe at the time, Madison viewed Washington's document as a clear encroachment upon Congress' exclusive authority to declare war. Underscoring the difficulties in assessing original intent and meaning in the Constitution, both then and now, Madison clari-fied his position by noting that Publius (Hamilton in *The Federalist*) had changed his mind about the nature of executive authority, one that was now supportive of Pacificus' position (Hamilton in the essays on the Proclamation of Neutrality) (Rakove, 356).

Such about-faces belie any fixed notions of the purity of constitutional interpretation. At Gettysburg, Lincoln ignored the Constitution altogether, what with its oblique references to slavery, choosing instead to ruminate on the Declaration and its contemporary relevance. As Young has written, the Federalists desired a limited popular government, whereas the Anti-Federalists wanted a popular limited government (Young, 69). The desire for a popular limited government was bought at a price at the Constitutional Convention, however – the acceptance of slavery. The development of states' rights arguments was thus difficult, if not impos-sible to extract from pro-slavery and, later, pro-Jim Crow policies.

If the Anti-Federalists lost the war over the Constitution's adoption, their less ardent but nevertheless stalwart cousins favoring it may have tempered the powers of the central government enough to make the Federalist victory a hollow one. Another way of putting it is to con-sider that part of the mythology of the Constitution is the historical fixation on "compromise." What's often left unsaid is that compromise does not necessarily facilitate equal outcomes; on the contrary, com-promise is often the means by which the stronger side secures the lion's share of its demands.

Southern slaveholding states may have threatened to walk out over perceived threats to slavery – but they didn't have to. Slavery was protected by the Three-Fifths Compromise and Fugitive Slave Act; small state power was protected in a Senate whose "majority" today represents a mere 18 percent of the United States' population.[2] The Senate's historic role in securing slavery, and later Jim Crow, is well documented. By the 1850s, six slave states had a free population with fewer people than Pennsylvania alone (Wills, 8, 2003). Coupled with the added gains in the House won for the South in Philadelphia in 1787, formal challenges to white supremacy were formidable, if not mathematically impossible. As Garry Wills has written, the "Deep South had made it clear that without this edge [the Three-Fifths Compromise] it would not ratify (it was a close call even with it)" (Wills, 59). The "compromise" made by northern states at the Constitutional Convention may otherwise be described as a capitulation – at least with respect to slavery. The South was the only party willing to walk out on the issue, and this proved decisive.

An unspoken byproduct of this arrangement was the relegation of enslaved black women to the role of power-generating sexual captives for whites, while southern white women were to be dual functionaries of white supremacy: gatekeepers of racial purity and instructors of republicanism to future male leaders. As Rogers Smith points out, "the Constitution left intact the state constitutions that denied women the franchise and other legal privileges" (Smith, 131). What was left was domesticity and its apolitical forms of subjugation. Indeed, the Framers' turn towards order fueled criticism and fears of the French Revolution and its aftermath in later years – including the fear of the "excesses" brought about by the nascent women's right movement as exemplified by Mary Wollstonecraft and her *Vindication of the Rights of Woman* (Smith, 148).

Today, most Americans are instructed to mark the nation's history through its presidential line of succession, one reminiscent of religious or dynastic lines whose origins connote legitimacy. The 44 faces spanning 45 presidencies are all male, and until very recently, all white. The American presidency, initially so concerned with precedent, became a precedent unto itself: namely, the institutional locus for marking time. This begs the question: How did Americans mark political time before the presidencies of Washington and Adams? It would seem that the Framers' uncertainty about the durability of the republic ("a republic if you can keep it," Benjamin Franklin is reported to have said to a woman inquiring about the nature of the new government in Philadelphia in 1787) drew attention away from prospective time and more towards the quality of virtue. As Anne Norton has noted, the presidency became a symbol of the nation – a unique constitutional bequest, as the Articles lacked such an executive (Norton, 1993). Republicanism in its own way was undone by public attention to the institution formerly viewed as least associated with self-government. The mixed government established and premised upon the writings of the "celebrated Montesquieu" and those small republics of the past did not become the focus of mass attention. That was the role of the American president. In the short span of the presidencies of George Washington and John Adams, the best and worst features of republicanism were present in ways highly instructive about the powers and perils inherent in the new institution.

Washington, Adams, and the Forging of National Identity

George Washington is not ordinarily associated with a political philosophy. In favor of a strong executive and national unity, he sought to convey an image above the partisan politics just beginning at the time. Associating himself with the virtuous and selfless Roman general Cincinnatus, Washington was nevertheless deeply influenced by the counsel of Alexander Hamilton, his Secretary of the Treasury, and by some accounts his de facto Prime Minister (Chernow, 289, 2004). Washington's closeness to Hamilton mattered a great deal as Hamilton was the critical figure within the nascent Federalist party. His policies on credit, the creation of a national bank, and executive power influenced the direction of national politics for many years to come. So, while Washington's posture was above partisanship, his chief aid was very much identified with a specific political ideology and party view.

The presidency evolved through a series of precedents – including control over the removal of his appointees. But it was the president's role in foreign policy and as commander-in-chief where the inclination to order was most evident. Both the Proclamation of Neutrality of 1793 and suppression of the Whiskey Rebellion in 1794 had the imprints of Hamilton's hand upon them. "Whenever the Government appears in arms it ought to appear like a *Hercules*," Hamilton wrote, underscoring his argument to Washington that rebellions had to be addressed with a powerful counter by the federal government (McDonald, 240, 1994). It remains the last and only occasion where an American president took to the field to command troops. Washington's use of the pardoning power during the rebellion has been seen as an example of its intended purpose as strategic tool for the restoration of political order. As Russell Riley has pointed out, Hamilton made it clear in *Federalist* No. 74 that this was a critical prospective feature of the new national executive's power:

> The principal argument for reposing the power of pardon in this case in the Chief Magistrate is this: in seasons of insurrection or rebellion, there are often critical moments when a well-timed offer of pardon to the insurgents or rebels may restore the tranquility of the commonwealth.
>
> (Riley, 13, 1999)

Presidential authority was thus employed early on to shape the politics of order – what Riley has called "nation-keeping." Another crucial element in mobilizing against the rebellion was the effort to keep the political allegiance of western settlers beyond the Alleghany Mountains (Frymer, 46). This was a considerable concern, one Washington outlined in his Farewell Address. The division between East and West was potentially as divisive as the one between North and South. The latter division was addressed at the Convention through accommodations to slavery, and this became the pattern over subsequent decades. The potential for such compromise with westerners was less straightforward, however; Hamilton's commitment to a national economic system involved the emergence of different sorts of institutions over time – including the emergence of the National Bank and an economy increasingly devoted to foreign trade and the protection of nascent eastern industries. In time, western expansion (and Indian removal) made western political power more formidable and helped establish the kinds of "attachments" to the national government the Framers had hoped would develop over time.

In addition, the Federalist expansionist view of national power was closely tied to interpretations of vast executive authority read into Article II of the Constitution. It was the vestment clause where Hamilton recognized the power of the president to exercise presidential authority not expressly confined to Article II. The first effort of consequence undertaken to infuse the executive branch with this kind of latitude was Washington's Proclamation of Neutrality. Issued in 1793 with war raging in Europe, Washington enlisted Hamilton to assist in finding a constitutional way to preserve American neutrality. What followed was one of the great constitutional debates – with Hamilton adopting the pseudonym of Pacificus in articles he would write in support of the measure, and James Madison, writing as Helvidius, in opposition. The so-called unitary theory of the executive was born, as "Hamilton based his argument on the 'broad and comprehensive ground' that the federative powers inhere in the executive," arguing he "could also have justified the proclamation solely on the constitutional clause charging the president to "take care that the laws be faithfully executed" (McDonald, 237).

The Proclamation would stand, and more importantly, one of the great movements towards executive power was born. It would not be until the Progressive Era, some 100 years later, that the United States would truly become an executive-centered republic; nevertheless, the audacious move to present the president as having authority to seemingly intrude upon Congress' explicit right to declare war was appalling to Madison – and to Jefferson – who had early on questioned the potential abuses of presidential authority.

What was achieved in the Proclamation of Neutrality, and in the repression of the Whiskey Rebellion, was mitigated by Washington's extraordinary decision to not seek a third term in 1796. Perhaps the greatest precedent set by him, Washington's decision steered the country away from the shoals of elected monarchy, reminding Americans that republicanism and unrestrained executive power were incompatible. The gesture would be a model for other, perhaps politically foolish but otherwise demonstrable, efforts to show disinterestedness in personal power. James Polk's pledge to not seek a second term, along with Teddy Roosevelt's (later lamented, and then recanted), were such examples of the thread of early American republican principles being adhered to many decades later.

Yet the presidential leviathan has proven to have many arms, and despite John Adams' one term in office, he nearly did irreparable harm to republican political thought with his effort to erase criticism of the president and his party from constitutional protections guarding the right to freedom of speech. The "alien" portion of the Alien and Sedition Acts likewise gave the president power to remove from the country "any foreigner deemed 'dangerous to the peace and safety of the United States'" (McDougall,

362). While the historian Walter McDougall plays down the relative significance of the legislation, Paul Frymer sees it as formative, having the "express purpose of keeping the non-English out." The Acts were a template of sorts, he writes, "no different from the twenty-first century, [when] numerous voices during the time objected to what they perceived as unclean vagabonds and convicts coming from Europe to take jobs" (Frymer, 62).

The Virginia and Kentucky Resolutions (1798), authored by James Madison and Thomas Jefferson respectively, argued that Congress had overstepped its bounds; Jefferson went as far as to claim the right of Kentucky (and other states) to nullify such acts that went beyond the powers and scope of Congress' constitutional role and powers. Jefferson saw in the Alien and Sedition Acts a grave threat to republican ideals. Nevertheless, Jefferson has been seen by some as sowing the seeds of secession by making a states' rights argument for nullification, one that at its core rejected the final power of the federal government. Charles Slack has written that "Jefferson bears some intellectual blame for the tragedies that states would inflict in seeking to preserve an economic system and a way of life that denied unalienable rights to millions of people" (Slack, 2016). The early American republic was thus confounded by efforts to constrain wayward executive power – a clear danger to representative government; its solution was but a doorway into deepening an already anti-democratic system of oppression, albeit one sanctioned by law. Such contradictions were at the heart of the American founding and perhaps no better illustrated than in the presidency of Thomas Jefferson.

Thomas Jefferson as President

Thomas Jefferson famously declined recording his time as America's third president on his gravestone upon his death. Other signature accomplishments, which he did deem worthy of remembrance, included his authoring the Declaration of Independence and statute of religious freedom in Virginia; he also included his founding of the University of Virginia. These all had the common feature of representing his republican ideals – opposition to tyranny, opposition to religious conformity, and finally, support for a well-educated and informed public. The presidency, ever a theoretical hobgoblin for Jefferson, was left to be a historic footnote.

But Thomas Jefferson was president for eight years, and in that time he helped radically alter the future of the fledgling democracy he was so instrumental in founding. His role in the creation and perpetuation of political parties, expansionist venture with the purchase of the Louisiana Territory, and ultimate advocacy of increased powers of the presidency[3] represented ideological shifts from his previous political stances. Nonetheless, as I will outline more specifically in Chapter Three, they were unmistakable features of the "Jeffersonian" politics often subordinated in discussions of Jefferson for the favored version of his "Virginian" (i.e. democratic) political philosophy. If, as James Young has argued (and I concede the point), "American radicals have always have had a soft spot for Jefferson," it is more because of his intellectual positions than his political machinations or policies as president (Young, 83).

Forrest McDonald's intellectual history of the American presidency reminds us that the Jeffersonian revolution was one held in deep skepticism by the Federalists – the de facto keepers of the revolutionary ruling political class to that point: "At stake, Hamilton said, was 'true liberty, property, order, religion and of course, *heads*'" (McDonald, 245). Hamilton's reference to heads was a nod to fears of Robespierrian politics making its way across the Atlantic, guillotine and all. Jefferson's opponents would be disappointed on this front. Jefferson did not, in fact, reduce government to its least effectual parts; on the contrary, he wielded executive authority shrewdly, passing more legislation through Congress than had Washington and Adams' administrations combined (McDonald, 247).

In addition to his $15 million purchase of Louisiana, of which only $2 million had been appropriated, Jefferson wielded presidential power unapologetically. He went to war in the Barbary Coast of North Africa without congressional approval (Congress was not in session), he issued an unpopular embargo, and "Jefferson and his lieutenants decided to use the weapon of impeachment to attack their most obnoxious foes on the Federalist bench" (Wilentz, 126, 2006). In short, while Jefferson assiduously adhered to symbolic gestures designed to republicanize the presidency ("it is better that I should not interfere," he said with respect to the impeachment of Justice Samuel Chase), he nevertheless was an active and energetic executive who used the office to his party's, and his own, political advantage (Wilentz, 126). Jefferson's embrace of executive power had considerable implications for racial power in the United States. As Rogers Smith notes:

[F]or Jefferson, acceptance of urbanism and industry in the east made it imperative that the U.S. expand its "empire of liberty" westward, increasing the domain of yeoman farmers. To do so again required wielding national powers expansively, as in the Louisiana Purchase, the Indian wars, and the negotiations with Spain that regained Florida under James Madison in 1819. Jefferson and his successors shelved their anxieties about centralized power and did what seemed necessary in these matters, trying peaceful means but proving willing to resort to force.

(Smith, 166)

The revolutionary impulses that were at the fore of Jefferson's thinking were thus largely subordinated during his presidency. Moreover, such impulses had little regard for the inclusion of women, blacks, and Native Americans. As the most widely perceived radical theorist among the founders, Jefferson's practical acceptance of order and national power represents the limitations of American political thought in the early republic. Jefferson's famous "wolf by the ear" statement in his letter concerning the Missouri Compromise in 1820 betrayed the greatest fear of the founders – the sense that white survival was linked to the preservation of slavery.

Jefferson had an uncanny inability to show empathy towards those enslaved. The idea that it was whites who were imperiled by slavery is a stark reminder that republican virtues were seldom, if ever, applied to blacks in American society during the founding period. On the contrary, fears of internal revolt, whether of the Federalist variety (seen in nascent democratic French revolutionary-inspired clubs) or Democratic-Republican (raised by the Haitian Revolution and black uprisings), marked the period. As Michael Hanchard notes:

The United States government responded to the French Revolution with the creation of the Alien and Sedition Acts of 1798 .... Regarding the Haitian Revolution, the US government was not only concerned with the spread of ideologies via elite discourse, but with the circulation of rebellious ideas among slave populations.

(Hanchard, 94, 2018)

The conservatism of the American Revolution and its aftermath was rooted in the quest to retain the racial hierarchy that had defined English settlement in the New World. Thomas Jefferson's unwillingness to move beyond the intellectual confines of a white racial republic was less a shortcoming than a conscious choice to assert and preserve American democratic principles along racial lines. James Young's view of Jefferson on this point is fairly representative of scholarship that is otherwise keen on asserting agency for America's early political leaders. With respect to slavery, however, Jefferson (as so many founders do) becomes "paralyzed"; his optimism "deserts him"; or most apologetically, "Jefferson, after all, was not an ogre, nor was he simply a hypocrite. He was a man of his time who shared the prejudices of his age" (Young, 108). It is hard to find other similarly tortured attempts to exculpate historic wrongs among historians and theorists alike than when probing the willful mind of American white racialists and supremacists.

Conclusion

The American Revolution fell prey to what ails almost every revolution: the counterbalancing act that seeks to restore order. The French, Russian, Mexican, Cuban, and Chinese revolutions are all of a piece in this regard, irrespective of their unique trajectories and historic contexts. But Americans tend to think of their revolution as ongoing, one that did not calcify under reactionary or anti-democratic forces. But this is because the American Revolution has long been stripped of its connections to white supremacy. It is written of in tomes as a precursor to "the rise of American democracy" – a kind of erasure of the hardening and expansion of slavery, not to mention its more restrictive and brutal forms in the Deep South. The expansion of white male suffrage in the 1820s and 1830s represented an undoubted gain for that global demographic; that it was accompanied by unimaginable human misery for native and black populations is seen as an afterthought, or part of a narrative of pending dissolution of the Union. As Paul Frymer makes plain:

> Perhaps the most critical consequence of land and settlement policies was how frequently the federal government attempted to manufacture racially specific outcomes – namely, the establishment of a white demographic stronghold, often with striking success and sometimes with equally notable failures – so as to enable the government to expand. The politics of race – and racism – was deeply embedded in settlement and territorial incorporation.
>
> (Frymer, 23)

Indeed, as Jill Lepore notes, "Jefferson deferred to his advisors" when finalizing the purchase of the Louisiana Territory, an act he deemed of questionable constitutionality. It would be, he thought, "the means of tempting all our Indians on the East side of the Mississippi to remove to the West" (Lepore, 171, 2018).

"What was the American Revolution?" John Adams asked. It was, it may be said, a particular form of revolution – a modern, shape-shifting, state-centralizing one, one with asymmetrical forms of liberty at its core. The shifts had to do with varying degrees of support for more local, as opposed to more national, power; the same was true for whether or not legislative, as opposed to executive, power would become more defining. Undergirding it all was an unwavering agreement that the new nation would be governed by a white male governing class, one with no entrée for blacks, indigenous peoples, or women. Thus began the movement from revolution to empire – one cloaked in the language of liberty.

Notes

1. https://founders.archives.gov/documents/Adams/99-02-02-6854.
2. "Why Even a Blue Wave Could Have Limited Gains," *New York Times*, August 20, 2018. www.nytimes.com/2018/08/20/opinion/midterms-democrats-republicans-blue-wave.html.
3. See McDonald, 246.

References

Hannah Arendt, *On Revolution* (New York: Penguin Classics, 2006).

Michael Burlingame, *The Inner World of Abraham Lincoln* (Urbana, IL: University of Illinois, 1994).

Michael X. Delli Carpini, "Black Panther Party: 1966–982," in I. Ness and J. Ciment (Eds.), *The Encyclopedia of Third Parties in America* (pp. 190–197) (Armonk, NY: Sharpe Reference, 2000). Retrieved from http://repository.upenn.edu/asc_papers/1

Ron Chernow, *Alexander Hamilton* (New York: Penguin Press, 2004).

Joseph J. Ellis, *Writing the Declaration of Independence* (New York: Vintage, 2015).

Paul Frymer, *Building an American Empire: The Era of Territorial and Political Expansion* (Princeton, NJ: Princeton University Press, 2017).

Alex Haley, *Roots: The Saga of an American Family* (Boston, MA: Da Capo Press, 1974).

Michael Hanchard, *The Spectre of Race: How Discrimination Haunts Western Democracy* (Princeton, NJ: Princeton University Press, 2018).

Harold James, *The Roman Predicament: How the Rules of International Order Create the Rules of Empire* (Princeton, NJ: Princeton University Press, 2008).

Ira Katznelson, *Freedom from Fear: The New Deal and the Origins of Our Time* (New York: W.W. Norton, 2013).

Isaac Kramnick and Theodore J. Lowi, *American Political Thought: A Norton Anthology* (New York: W.W. Norton, 2009).

Jill Lepore, *These Truths: A History of the United States* (New York: W.W. Norton, 2018).

Theodore J. Lowi, "Bend Sinister: How the Constitution Saved the Republic and Lost Itself: The 2008 James Madison Lecture," *PS: Political Science and Politics*, 42(1), 3–9, 2009.

Richard K. Matthews, *The Radical Politics of Thomas Jefferson: A Revisionist View* (Lawrence, KS: University Press of Kansas, 1984).

Forrest McDonald, *The American Presidency: An Intellectual History* (Lawrence, KS: University Press of Kansas, 1994).

Walter A. McDougall, *Freedom Just around the Corner: A New American History, 1585–1828* (New York: HarperCollins, 2004).

Wilson Carey McWilliams, *Redeeming Democracy in America* (Patrick J Deneen and Susan J. McWilliams, Eds.) (Lawrence, KS: University Press of Kansas, 2011).

Anne Norton, *Republic of Signs: Liberal Theory and American Popular Culture* (Chicago, IL: University of Chicago Press, 1993).

Jack Rakove, *Revolutionaries: A New History of the Invention of America* (Boston, MA: Houghton Mifflin Harcourt, 2010).

Russell Riley, *The Presidency and the Politics of Racial Inequality* (New York: Columbia University Press, 1999).

Charles Slack, *Liberty's First Crisis: Adams, Jefferson, and the Misfits Who Saved Free Speech* (New York: Grove Press, 2016).

Rogers Smith, *Civic Ideals: Conflicting Visions of Citizenship in U.S. History* (New Haven, CT: Yale University Press, 1997).

Charles C. Thach, Jr., *The Creation of the Presidency, 1775–1779: A Study in Constitutional History* (Indianapolis, IN: Liberty Fund, 2010).

Alexis de Tocqueville, *Democracy in America* (Harvey Mansfield and Delba Winthrop, Eds.) (Chicago, IL: University of Chicago Press, 2000).

Sean Wilentz, *The Rise of Democracy in American Democracy: Jefferson to Lincoln* (New York: W.W. Norton, 2006).

Garry Wills, *Negro President: Jefferson and the Slave Power* (New York: Houghton Mifflin, 2003).

Gordon S. Wood, *The Radicalism of the American Revolution* (New York: Alfred A. Knopf, 1992).

James P. Young, *Reconsidering American Liberalism: The Troubled Odyssey of the Liberal Idea* (Boulder, CO: Westview Press, 1996).

CHAPTER THREE
JEFFERSON'S "EMPIRE OF LIBERTY": 1800–1850

Introduction

Thomas Jefferson's election to the presidency in 1800 is said to have
represented a revolutionary break from the Federalist theory of government. Yet, over the course of the next half-century, his vision of
a nation anchored by the rule of local governments, civic virtue, and
the protection of personal liberties was severely challenged. American
national development was increasingly marked by the growing power
of the federal government and a westward expansion that brought to
the fore powerful opposing interpretations of both liberty and citizenship. By mid-century, the United States, having doubled its size under
Jefferson's purchase of the Louisiana Territory as president, was on the
brink of being severed along opposing ideological lines. Slavery was
the critical question, as it had been at the Constitutional Convention –
and the ensuing progression of national compromises could only stave
off a solution to Jefferson's zero-sum equation gleaned from the Missouri Compromise in 1820. Upon learning of the scheme to balance
the slaveholding and non-slaveholding power of the states in Congress,
Jefferson, nearing the end of his life, said America faced the choice of
"Justice or [white] self-preservation."[1]

The prospect of racial annihilation as a plausible outcome of the
decidedly *Herrenvolk* (ethnically defined) nature of the early American

republic was not a concern unique to Jefferson. Alexis de Tocqueville would later formulate a similar accounting of American life (he purposely left the nation's race relations outside the purview of his discussion of democracy, seeing it as an undemocratic feature of his investigation). Indeed, Tocqueville painted an uncharacteristically bleak portrait of "the future of the three races in America" in *Democracy in America* (first published in French in 1835), offering that at best, the indigenous Native American population would be exterminated, with blacks and whites likely partners in a destructive and pathological struggle – one for supremacy (for whites), and the other for personhood (for blacks). Reflecting on the atrocities committed against Native Americans during his sojourn in America, Tocqueville was deeply and uncommonly pessimistic:

> [These are] great evils; and it must be added that they appear to me to be irremediable. I believe that the Indian nations of North America are doomed to perish, and that whenever the Europeans shall be established on the shores of the Pacific Ocean, that race of men will have ceased to exist.
>
> (Tocqueville, 312, 2000)

The incompatibility of white supremacy with black and Indian personhood defined the parameters of a larger national struggle for settling the newly acquired western territories. Only in the states established by the Northwestern Ordinance was there a clear delineation of a nonracial commitment to citizenship. The 1787 agreement between the states and federal government included a ban on slavery. This fact would be a vital part of Abraham Lincoln's case against slavery as a natural guiding principle of American statehood. At Cooper Union in New York in 1860, Lincoln would retrospectively invalidate the notion that the United States had been from the start, a white man's republic. The prohibition against slavery in the northwestern territories was a critical feature of his argument (Holzer, 2004). But Lincoln, however artfully, was also selectively excising much of nineteenth-century political history, whose climactic event up to that point had been a war waged against Mexico, one deeply motivated by the desire to expand slavery. Lincoln argued against that war, as had abolitionists and the early Transcendentalists, including Ralph Waldo Emerson; but theirs was a losing argument (as all arguments opposing slavery's expansion had been). Indeed, Henry David Thoreau's night in jail in 1844 for refusing to pay Massachusetts taxes as a sign of his opposition to the war and slavery's expansion would become the basis of his influential essay "On Civil Disobedience" (Hall, 437, 2018). Such dissent may have been unsuccessful at the time, but it would inspire future generations of civil rights leaders, including Dr. Martin Luther King, Jr. and Bayard Rustin.

With respect to slavery, Lincoln and the early abolitionists were proponents of separation – the colonization of blacks to Africa upon emancipation. This had not been very different from Jefferson's view expressed in his "fire bell in the night" letter to John Holmes, equating black freedom with white annihilation. Jefferson wrote to Holmes teasing out the possibility, however remote, of "emancipation and *expatriation*," a view presaging Lincoln's own best hopes, up until very late in his life. This was the "enlightened" view of black liberation at the time, one very much tied to the practical politics of the period, as cheap and plentiful western lands were ripe for settlement, linking white male suffrage to Indian removal and black slavery. Jefferson was as unhopeful as Tocqueville would prove to be:

> I can say with conscious truth that there is not a man on earth who would sacrifice more than I would, to relieve us from this heavy reproach, in any *practicable* way. The cession of that kind of property, for so it is misnamed, is a bagatelle which would not cost me in a second thought, if, in that way, a general emancipation and *expatriation* could be effected: and, gradually, and with due sacrifices, I think it might be. But, as it is, we have the wolf by the ear, and we can neither hold him, nor safely let him go.[2]

The expansion of democratic politics, so esteemed by historians of "the Age of Jackson" was also, ironically enough, contingent upon the denial of political rights to women, who increasingly saw their apolitical status (with rare exception in the states) as cause for protest and political organization. Democracy required time, and the demands for both domestic and manual labor followed the classical Greek model, co-joining slavery with the political sequestration of women.

The opening chapter of James Fennimore Cooper's *The Last of the Mohicans* (1826) painted the *Herrenvolk* idyll quite well. The setting of the French and Indian War quite literally, colors the novel with an Edenic, pre-Independence world of possibilities. The American nation was to emerge out of a contested milieu of Anglo, French, and Indian confrontations. As the Book of Genesis is in many ways a "genetic" and ancestral narrative of Adam's family history, so too is Cooper's opening one of genetic origins and possibilities. Two sisters – Alice, with a "dazzling complexion" and "fair golden hair," is accompanied on a journey by the mixed-race Cora (simply described as "the other" with a "complexion not brown") (Cooper, 10, 2011). As the Indian scout Magua runs past the women seated in their carriage, it is Cora who betrays an attraction for him, drawn to his dark form in a lustful gaze. Alice, on the other hand, gasps with revulsion. This is Cooper's impressionistic sketch of the early American sexual-racial template for survival. Cora's mixed-race status renders her incapable of producing a new (and pure) world of republican freedom. This is literary hindsight, of course, as all founding myths must be. But Cooper's vision, at least in its backdrop, illustrates a first principle found in Jacksonian America: all mulattoes must be tragic (as is Cora's end in the novel). The hue of the cheeks of women, from Jefferson's *Notes on the State of Virginia* to Cooper's *Mohicans*, must be white – "pink" for Jefferson (as opposed to "the monotonous veil of black" the master of Monticello found in African American women). Cooper's literary coloration was "bright and delicate."

It is only Herman Melville who challenges the early literary presumption of racial purity drawn in this way, labeling the "butterfly cheeks" of young [white] girls "a deceit" in *Moby-Dick*. For Melville, humanity is ultimately united by the "charnel house within" – the commonality of our individual deaths. Whiteness, properly understood, exists in the imagination at best. At worst, it is the springboard for the nation's demise ("Wonder ye then at the fiery hunt?") (Melville, 197, 1979).

For Melville, the hunt alluded to at the end of his chapter "The Whiteness of the Whale" was in part emblematic of the hunt for Mexico, for more slave territories, for greater wealth, power, and national prestige. Melvillian political thought, transcendent as it was, was unfortunately like that of his character Starbuck, an eloquent but minor democratic note of the times, one drowned out by the push for

"Manifest Destiny." Starbuck muses about killing Ahab – "Shall this crazed old man be tamely suffered to drag a whole ship's company down to doom with him?" – but he is paralyzed against doing so. Melville is keen on presenting how desperate the lost moment is, as there is no other opposition to Ahab's tyranny on board the *Pequod* (Melville, 517).

Yet national greatness was an objective questioned from the beginning, at least as far back as Virginia's constitutional ratifying convention in 1787. There, Patrick Henry said, "Some way or other we must be a great and mighty empire" (Wooton, 33, 2003) He did not mean it as a compliment. Before long, Jefferson negotiated a fusion between Henry's coveted, but losing, national focus on "liberty" (at least white male liberty) and the Federalist desire to create a powerful nation. And so Jefferson's seemingly incompatible coupling of founding conceits was born. The United States was now to become an "Empire of Liberty."

Revolution Betrayed? The Election of 1800 and Beyond

The election of Thomas Jefferson was the first in modern history where a democratically elected political party took power from another. Highlighting the theme of national unity, Jefferson wrote in his inaugural address that "We are all Republicans, we are all Federalists." Where Washington's Farewell Address prioritized the ethnocultural unity of the nation ("with slight shades of difference, you have the same religion, manners, habits, and political principles"), Jefferson sought to promote a national unity based upon a commitment to limited self-government.[3]

Jefferson came to power in most unusual fashion, having defeated Aaron Burr, his prospective Vice President, through a vote in the House of Representatives, owing to a tie in the Electoral College. The delicate nature of American democracy required presidential rhetorical pledges to unity and republican heterodoxy. But Jefferson's Inaugural revealed the fingerprints of his attempt at a radical break from Federalist power and its emphasis on a large, strong central government. "I know, indeed," Jefferson said, "that some honest men fear that republican government cannot be strong, that this government is not strong enough." But what made America strong, he argued, was its people's attachment to the rule of law, not the might of its rulers.[4] Jefferson aspired to a government more durable and stronger than the one provided in the Articles of Confederation, but also one far less energetic than desired by his Federalist rivals.

This rejection of Hamiltonian government became most perplexing given Jefferson's decision to unilaterally take it upon himself, presumably as an unspoken power of his constitutional authority, to purchase the enormity of the Louisiana Territory from France in 1803. The once-imagined sparsely populated, agrarian nation of small farmers, closely tied to their government in little ward republics, became almost overnight a massive continental state with an imperial nature imprinted upon it just 20 years after the Peace of Paris. The political scientist Ted Lowi, echoing any number of skeptics over the years, thought the purchase was of questionable constitutionality at best. He was not alone. So did Jefferson.[5]

Jefferson's act virtually assured slavery's continuation into the newly acquired western territories. Dubbed a "Negro President" by his critics, as the historian Garry Wills has noted (owing to Jefferson's election based on the difference in additional electoral votes cast in the South from the Three-Fifths Compromise), Jefferson singlehandedly diminished the prospects of the institution's demise (Wills, 2003). As the historian Robin Blackburn pointed out:

> The Louisiana Purchase confirmed that the United States was an empire as well as a republic and it confirmed that slaveholders would have their own reserved space within that empire. Because he was President, because of his historic role, and because he was a Virginian, Jefferson was the only man who could have prevented this development.
>
> (Kennedy, 2003)

While Gordon Wood and others have argued that Jefferson's use of the term "Empire of Liberty" was not an expression of imperialistic intent in the conventional sense of empire's meaning, the term was fraught with troubling attachments even in the early nineteenth century. And Jefferson's use must also be understood as validating a certain kind of empire, perhaps new in the world (from Jefferson's point of view): one that would carry the blessings of self-government with it throughout its expanse. Of course, this was very much in keeping with Napoleonic sentiments of *liberté*, as France sought to justify its growing empire as an extension of revolutionary values. That the Louisiana Purchase was made possible because of Napoleon's financial troubles owing to the growing ferocity of the black slave revolts and burgeoning revolution on Sainte-Domingue cannot be lost in any assessment of Jeffersonian political thought. Indeed, one might correctly attach Jefferson to Andrew Jackson in terms of his uplifting an ethos of white settler expansionist policy, as much as for the more readily employed comparison of his support for mass democracy.

That the virtues of local government were intertwined with the near exclusivity of white citizenship from the nation's inception left the initial Anti-Federalist and later Democratic Party's position on states' rights both morally and philosophically compromised. Where Andrew Jackson would espouse an anti-centrist governing philosophy, it would be on matters pertaining to Indian Removal (1831), economic populism (opposition to the National Bank), and the authority of the executive branch to lead (as in his fight with his former Vice President John C. Calhoun in opposing South Carolina's attempt at nullification over tariff policy). Jacksonian democracy epitomized white nationalist politics, with the chief opposition coming from John Marshall's court, whose imposition of institutional constraints was largely successful on questions of constitutional interpretation regarding the role of the federal government; they were otherwise impotent with respect to the rights of Native Americans and questions of slavery (at least up until 1817) (Goldstein, 20, 2017).

The period was thus one of tilted democratic development – the surge in white electoral rights and liberties with western expansion coinciding with the forced migration of Native Americans to barren settlements in the West. Slavery soon followed the path of this forced migration, ensuring a chokehold of political power for the South up until mid-century, with Jefferson but the first of numerous "Negro" presidents.

With no real opposition party confronting the newly evolved Democratic Party, the "Era of Good Feelings" was characterized as much by religious zeal as it was by politics. The Second Great Awakening infused morally based arguments into political debate, moving national discourse away from more secular, Enlightenment premises. While fervent in their anti-slavery position, those advocating abolition were still more inclined to support colonization, while those who invoked biblical theories of white racial superiority argued that the institution of slavery had "improved" the status of blacks in the New World. Politically, the emergent Whig Party was split along pro and anti-slavery lines, further weakening the political forces that otherwise might have struck a blow against slavery's expansion. As the abolitionist movement moved away from colonization to black political equality, some Whigs, like Abraham Lincoln, staked out a middle ground, one neither abolitionist nor expansionist. Between the Missouri Compromise (1820) and the Compromise of 1850, slavery only grew in influence, along with the two opposing views of the institution's place within American society.

With the death of Jefferson in 1826 and Andrew Jackson's election in 1828, post-revolutionary forces had grown to define a new set of challenges and opportunities for American democracy. The role of the national government had grown in its power – western settlement, banking interests, and a second war with England all played a role in moving the country away from the civic republican ideal of the nation's founders. But there remained formidable opposition to the centralizing forces of the period. These were critically arrayed against the first wave of mass European immigration, movements to empower women, more radical calls for emancipation, and those voices calling for restraint against the impulse for territorial conquest. These were not new debates, but they had been made perceptibly more volatile, if not intractable – a byproduct of Jefferson's compromises with his earliest political thought. With slavery removed from national discourse quite literally by Congress with a forced gag rule on debate, the silence over the deepest divide in national political life allowed for a period of relative national unity over other questions, with Congress and House Speaker Henry Clay playing an outsized role in these matters.

The period was thus defined by the Jacksonian politics of white democratic populism – a racialized nationalism buoyed by territorial claims on Native, Spanish, and formerly French lands. The intellectual repudiation of Jacksonian politics was political Whiggery and the emergence of the Transcendentalist movement, highlighted by the writings of Ralph Waldo Emerson and Henry David Thoreau. Importantly, the movement not only espoused a reorientation towards nature and a cosmology of self-directedness; it also was committed to a vision of human equality that defied the period's racial and gender politics.[6]

Furthering the Transcendentalist message, the writings of Margaret Fuller presented a political vision of gender equality that was a forerunner of the Suffragist Movement that followed. The abolitionists soon embraced the push for women's rights, although the relationship between the two movements would on occasion clash (Bailey, Viens, and White, 135, 2013).

Perhaps no one would meld the Whig ideal of constitutional democracy with the Transcendental ideal as well as Abraham Lincoln. But even the more moderate Whig appeals to preserving the Union could not prevent movement towards secession and Civil War; only the unprecedented and shocking bloodletting that ensued presented the occasion for a rethinking of national priorities. Despite the sectional struggles that resulted from westward expansion and the difficulty of balancing political power in Congress, nationalists embraced war with Mexico – an evident, yet popularly lauded, betrayal of the Jeffersonian impulse towards a small, peaceful, democratic state.

Black Rebellion and Nation-Keeping

When Thomas Jefferson expressed opposition to King George III's "exciting domestic insurrections" in the American colonies in the Declaration of Independence, he gave voice to the fear of black revolt in the United States. That fear, present from the founding, grew to shape not only national politics, but also American political thought. Five years later, in his *Notes on the State of Virginia*, Jefferson reiterated the sentiment, this time referencing the role of memory in prospective black violence:

> It will probably be asked, Why not retain and incorporate the blacks into the state, and thus save the expence of supplying, by importation of white settlers, the vacancies they will leave? Deep rooted prejudices entertained by the whites; ten thousand recollections, by the blacks, of the injuries they have sustained; new provocations; the real distinctions which nature has made; and many other circumstances, will divide us into parties, and produce convulsions which will probably never end but in the extermination of the one or the other race.
>
> (Lewis and Onuf, 265, 1999)

Such "recollections" were believed to be the spurs to violent action, emanating from an uncontrollable disposition on the part of blacks to exact revenge upon their former masters. Not unlike his view of white insurrection in the case of Shays' Rebellion, Jefferson saw black rebellion as a wholly just and rational act. "I tremble for my country," Jefferson wrote in *Notes on Virginia*, "when I remember God is just; that his justice cannot sleep forever" (Lewis and Onuf, 265).

The demographic makeup of the United States – an incomparably young nation with an enslaved racial minority largely concentrated in one portion of the country – was a critical factor in American political development for the better part of the nineteenth century. The harshest laws and more brutal forms of chattel slavery were located in the Deep South, where the numbers of enslaved Africans reached levels near those of whites (and in some counties, surpassed them). The intensification of this relationship between fear and repression was heightened by the situation on the island of Saint Domingue, where the colonial French-administered portion of the island – Haiti – was swept up in revolutionary fervor, and ultimately, independence.

The cost of black liberation in the New World proved to be a bloodletting of the white colonial class of Haiti. The implications were not simply theoretical for southerners, though a formidable political theory of white supremacy was advanced. A new and modern form of racialized statecraft was given the veneer of intellectual heft through the writings and speeches of John C. Calhoun, whose racist reasoning was readily coupled with southern arguments for states' rights. His speech "Slavery as a Positive Good" was perfectly tailored to the needs of southern planter society, as both a counter to northern industrial interests and the cause of abolition.

> We of the South will not, cannot, surrender our institutions. To maintain the existing relations between the two races, inhabiting that section of the Union, is indispensable to the peace and happiness of both .... Be it good or bad, [slavery] has grown up with our society and institutions, and is so interwoven with them that to destroy it would be to destroy us as a people. But let me not be understood as admitting, even by implication, that the existing relations between the two races in the slaveholding States is an evil: – far otherwise; I hold it to be a good, as it has thus far proved itself to be to both, and will continue to prove so if not disturbed by the fell spirit of abolition.
>
> (Calhoun, 357, 2017)

Aside from the idea of slavery as a "positive good," southerners also justified the continuation of the institution as a bulwark against black violence against whites. The Gabriel Prosser (1800), Denmark Vesey (1822), and Nat Turner (1831) plots and revolts were illustrative links in a chain of anti-black politics justifying racial repression, by both the state and its citizens. It is worth noting that Abraham Lincoln's first public address of consequence, his speech to the Young Men's Lyceum (1838), was in response to the public burning of a black man named Francis J. McIntosh by a mob of whites in St. Louis. McIntosh's murder aroused the white abolitionist editor Elijah P. Lovejoy, who condemned the attack as an act of "savage barbarity." McIntosh's "crime," for which he was imprisoned and later removed from his cell to be summarily executed, remains in some historic dispute. But the justification for it at the time was a purported act of violence on his part. American extrajudicial violence – terror – had its roots not only in slavery and settler conquest, it was also steeped in retributive notions of justice for even the suggestion of violence against whites. It was not the scourge of slavery that Lincoln focused on in his address, but rather the growing tendency towards lawlessness:

> There is no grievance that is a fit object of redress by mob law. In any case that arises, as for instance, the promulgation of abolitionism, one of two positions is necessarily true; that is, the thing is right within itself, and therefore deserves the protection of all law and all good citizens; or, it is wrong, and therefore proper to be prohibited by legal enactments; and in neither case, is the interposition of mob law, either necessary, justifiable, or excusable.
>
> (Foner, 28, 2010)

As Rogers Smith and Desmond King have argued, America's racial orders were woven into institutional practices suited to the historical moment; and yet the founding itself created, argued for, and pushed to sustain a de facto racial order that was routinely challenged by black and Indian populations from the very beginning. The "positive good" Calhoun suggested as the rationale for slavery was steeped in pseudo-Christian theology – a kind of Providential claim on black lives that were enriched somehow in the furnace of the American slave experience. The most basic counter, of course, was the responses of enslaved (and free) blacks themselves – especially those literate and biblically trained. Such counters were part of a cyclical process of oppression, revolt, (state) terror, intensification of legal and extralegal repression, and then revolt. Racial quiescence was never fully attained, though black and Indian populations were unmistakably the principal victims of this ritual cycle. For Lincoln, American democratic norms, precious and ever fleeting, also suffered in the process.

Tocqueville understood early on that a warped psychological dimension of identification between master and slave buttressed the material nature of American slavery. Where Native Americans were able to retain a semblance of autonomy both geographically and psychically from whites, blacks were more deeply connected to whites through chattel slavery. This proximity insisted upon black self-rejection and an unattainable longing for white identity. It was, perhaps, the earliest description of black double-consciousness, at least from an outsider; and it foreshadowed the kind of social analysis found over a century later in Franz Fanon's *Black Skin, White Masks*:

> The Negro makes a thousand fruitless efforts to insinuate himself among men who repulse him; he conforms to the tastes of his oppressors, adopts their opinions, and hopes by imitating them to form a part of their community. Having been told from infancy that his race is naturally inferior to that of the whites, he assents to the proposition and is ashamed of his own nature. In each of his features he discovers a trace of slavery, and if it were in his power, he would willingly rid himself of everything that makes him what he is.
>
> (Tocqueville, 373, 2013)

The great irony for Tocqueville was that black identification with whites created the possibility for group survival, whereas for Indians, psychological independence and an unwillingness to adapt (at least in Tocqueville's eyes) to Anglo culture meant certain extermination. Thus, one of the more profound expositions in American political thought carried with it another zero-sum game of racial hierarchy.

Tocqueville did not draw much on the experience of black rebellion, as Arthur Kaledin has pointed out (Kaledin, 2011). Nor did he devote much time to the suffrage or nascent labor movements of the period. But he did speak to the central American conflict of race, given slavery's inherent incompatibility with democratic norms – something that, at the time, very few associated with the need for gender equality. That black rebellion and revolutionary potentiality (related to Haiti) escaped his discussion of race in America represents a considerable hole in Tocqueville's understanding of how race and slavery worked in the early to mid-nineteenth century. Nevertheless, he did capture an important dimension of racial oppression – first acknowledging that the American slave system was not a natural outgrowth of inherited white superiority, as Calhoun and others argued; on the contrary, Tocqueville saw slavery's continuation in an otherwise democratic society as a fundamentally brutish capitulation on the part of whites to political power and greed.

It is no small irony, then, that among the most incisive reflections related to American political thought and race at mid-century, *Democracy in America* came not from the mind of an American, but rather from a youthful outsider, interested in his country avoiding those anti-democratic elements of social and political life of a nation he otherwise wished his country to emulate.

Suffrage and Citizenship

While he did not believe "men had any business" in Seneca Falls, and if present, "should take back benches and wrap themselves in silence," Frederick Douglass, an early supporter of women's suffrage, was one of the few men in attendance at the historic 1848 convention. Douglass drew a clear line between his opposition to slavery and the rights of women to be equal citizens, saying that "all good causes are mutually helpful" (Douglass, 706–710, 1999). His 1888 reflections on his participation at the event organized by Elizabeth Cady Stanton, some 40 years later, reveal the slow march of progress on the issue, as it would be another 20 years before women would gain the right to vote.

Early American notions of gender equality took the form of what would later be called "republican motherhood," an argument for the domestic and quite limited freedom of women to instruct their children in the precepts of democratic life within the home. This private instruction was to be advanced in the civic arena by sons, who would contribute to the republic as a result of the education and moral values received within the home. As Linda Kerber has pointed out, this was an Enlightenment-informed worldview, one largely traced to John Locke (Kerber, 17, 1997). Republican motherhood (a term coined by Kerber) emerged as a response to the more radical political ideas of Mary Wollstonecraft, who viewed female domesticity as an affront to women's basic humanity:

> It is a measure of the conservatism of the Revolution that women remained on the periphery of the political community; it is possible to read the subsequent political history of women in America as the story of women's efforts to accomplish for themselves what the Revolution had failed to do. From the time of the Revolution to our own day, the language of Republican Motherhood remains the most readily accepted – though certainly not the most radical justification for women's political behavior.
>
> (Kerber, 12)

Early feminists worked to extend the rights of women beyond the private sphere. While Abigail Adams' letter to John Adams (attending the Philadelphia convention for the drafting of the Declaration of Independence at the time) admonished him and the male delegates in attendance to "Remember the Ladies," this movement for more public rights, including suffrage, did not gain popular support until the 1830s and 1840s. It was not coincidental that the abolitionist movement grew in influence during this period, as religious and ethical arguments for the full humanity and citizenship for blacks compelled similar considerations and arguments for the equality of women. While political progress related to these twin movements was uneven and staggered, the roots of later success, for feminists and abolitionists alike, could be tied to this period.

As the historian Ibram X. Kendi has shown, black and white women's responses to slavery and the Fugitive Slave Act at mid-century gave rise to calls for full equality irrespective of race or gender. Indeed, "many of the early White women suffragists had spent years in the trenches of abolitionism, oftentimes recognizing the interlocking nature of American racism and sexism" (Kendi, 191, 2016). After Seneca Falls, the pace of the women's movement intensified, with the work of Harriet Beecher Stowe, Frances Dana Gage, and Sojourner Truth all fashioning political and religious arguments toward the end of gender inequality. Elizabeth Cady Stanton's Declaration of Sentiments at Seneca echoed the Declaration of Independence in affirming the universality of political equality – while advancing the still contentious point that women were the intellectual, physical, and social equals of men. The document was radical in its efforts to upend traditional and repressive roles accorded to women; by using the format and language of the Declaration of Independence, it linked American male political actors as agents of a similar kind of oppression that beset the colonists some three-quarters of a century before:

> The history of mankind is a history of repeated injuries and usurpations on the part of man toward woman, having in direct object the establishment of an absolute tyranny over her. To prove this, let facts be submitted to a candid world.
>
> He has never permitted her to exercise her inalienable right to the elective franchise.
>
> He has compelled her to submit to laws, in the formation of which she had no voice.
>
> He has withheld from her rights which are given to the most ignorant and degraded men – both natives and foreigners.[7]

Unfortunately, the case for women's rights would echo other similarly troubling political rationales throughout American history: namely the juxtaposition of perceived "less desirable" groups – in this instance, "foreigners" – against those viewed as more worthy.[8]

In her effort to further the women's movement, Sojourner Truth emphasized the racial oppression of black women, who had been, and remained, perhaps the most alienated persons in American society. "Ain't I a woman?" Truth asked at the Ohio Women's Rights Convention in 1851. Truth's question presented an ironic, multifaceted view of the interlocking dimensions of racial and gender identity. White feminists viewed being "merely" a woman as a form of acquiescence to oppressive masculine norms; for Truth, womanhood for whites nevertheless conferred a level of benevolent treatment – a kind of humanity, reduced though it was, that was divorced from the experience of black women. Truth's query (always the best of philosophical redirections) contained a powerful subtext: black women were neither fully human, nor were they women. They resided at best in some intermediary state, not far removed from Jefferson's assessment in *Notes on Virginia*, which rendered them more appropriate for the ardor of the "Oranatan" than human males.

In a prescient passage from his chapter on "The Future of the Three Races in America," Alexis de Tocqueville illustrated an early version of racial triangulation, later theorized by the political scientist Claire Jean Kim.[9] Tocqueville's portrait was of his experience in Alabama when happening upon a white girl, cared for by a black woman, who was otherwise engaged with an Indian woman. The trio, all of whom lacked full social standing in America based upon their status as females, nevertheless represented different placements within America's racial hierarchy. The passage is worth reviewing at length:

> I remember that while I was traveling through the forests which still cover the state of Alabama, I arrived one day at the log house of a pioneer. I did not wish to penetrate into the dwelling of the American, but retired to rest myself for a while on the margin of a spring, which was not far off, in the woods. While I was in this place, an Indian woman appeared, followed by a Negress, and holding by the hand a little white girl of five or six years, whom I took to be the daughter of the pioneer. A sort of barbarous luxury set off the costume of the Indian; rings of metal were hanging from her nostrils and ears, her hair, which was adorned with glass beads, fell loosely upon her shoulders; and I saw that she was not married, for she still wore that necklace of shells which the bride always deposits on the nuptial couch. The Negress was clad in squalid European garments. All three came and seated themselves upon the banks of the spring; and the young Indian, taking the child in her arms, lavished upon her such fond caresses as mothers give, while the Negress endeavored, by various little artifices, to attract the attention of the young Creole. The child displayed in her slightest gestures a consciousness of superiority that formed a strange contrast with her infantine weakness; as if she received the attentions of her companions with a sort of condescension. The Negress was seated on the ground before her mistress, watching her smallest desires and apparently divided between an almost maternal affection for the child and servile fear; while the savage, in the midst of her tenderness, displayed an air of freedom and pride which was almost ferocious.
>
> (Joshi, 15, 1999)

Again, for Tocqueville, the psychological dimension of slavery is rendered as significant as the physical and political nature of the institution. The bas relief of racial oppression is made clearer by attending to the manner in which African, Indigenous, and Anglo identities become foci of external power dynamics. The fact that the three are female demonstrates the unequal effects of racial identity on social status; even age lacks its ordinary significance as a barometer for elevated status, as the white girl remains the central figure of the scene around whom the other women orbit.

Later in the century, Douglass and other blacks would argue the case for the primacy of Negro suffrage before women's. The rationale was that the American political order could not absorb both causes simultaneously, and that the historical circumstances of black oppression – slavery – had necessitated the completion of black rights before insisting on the same for women. The debate was fraught with tension and animosity between the two movements at times, particularly as the 15th Amendment was circumvented after Reconstruction with the advent of Jim Crow laws and black disenfranchisement. Black women were double-victims in this period of stasis with respect to women's suffrage and the retrenchment of black male voting rights. The history of the nineteenth century proved to be one largely defined by conflict over the spoils of white men who were the chief beneficiaries of Jefferson's Empire of Liberty, rather than the more optimistic hope for "a new birth of freedom" promised by Lincoln.

Jeffersonian political thought may have allowed for the potentiality of black, native, and women's equality with white males, but it offered no political program, nor did the territorial expansion of the republic improve its chances. Indeed, expansion intensified the contraction of rights. Abolitionists and suffragists alike were confronted with a remarkably different country in 1850 than the one they labored in during the early Jackson era. The nation's borders had expanded to encompass half of Mexico's territory, won through annexation and war; the United States was becoming an increasingly industrial nation, dependent upon cheap labor and the many new immigrants who provided it. With westward expansion the driving force of national politics, the liberties so coveted by the revolutionary generation were no longer a preeminent concern. The push for land and continental – and indeed, hemispheric – dominance (as indicated in Monroe's precedent-setting doctrine in 1823) further marginalized the status of anyone but white Protestant males. None bore the brunt of this messianic movement more than American Indians, whose land, lives, and liberties were discarded as readily as the American government's promises to them during the period. The Empire of Liberty had become a settler nation, a White Republic – a *Herrenvolk* democracy defined chiefly by whiteness as the sin qua non for political and social status. At mid-century, Herman Melville could only lament that "Not yet have we solved the incantation of this whiteness, and learned why it appeals with such power to the soul" (Babb, 1998).

Settlement Nation

It was the Black Hawk War of 1832 that gave the US government the most proximate impetus for its Indian Removal policy under Andrew Jackson. But forced Indian removal from their lands had long been de facto British, and later, American policy in one form or another. Jackson's military participation in the Seminole Wars in Florida during 1816–1819 was but of a piece of this history. A Second (1835–1842) and Third Seminole War (1855–1858) would be fought, with related forced migrations of Seminole, Creek, Chickasaw, Choctaw, and Cherokee tribes westward. As Paul Frymer has shown, "by the time of the Removal Act of 1830, the bulk of Indian removal had already occurred" (Frymer, 114, 2017). The United States' status as a white settler nation became a legal reality in 1841 with the Senate voting 37 to 1 to define settlers as "white" (Frymer, 139).

Much of American political thought on the question of US–Indian relations has been focused on the constitutional crisis created by Jackson's refusal to adhere to Chief Justice John Marshall's ruling to protect the legal status of Cherokee lands in the *Worcester v. Georgia* (1832) decision. Yet the imbroglio over Indian rights invoked critical discussion about the nature of citizenship, the relationship of property rights to color, and the power of the government to make war against those it categorized as savage. In point of fact, the most benevolent public policy advocates of the period favored forms of relocation and colonization for indigenous and African peoples in the United States, creating the parameters of a nation favorably disposed towards, and engaging in, a republican form of ethnic cleansing. "It is impossible to destroy men with more respect for the laws of humanity," Alexis de Tocqueville observed at the time (Tocqueville, 325, 2000).

The greatest period of the expansion of democratic rights in the modern era, marked by universal (white) male suffrage, was thus enabled by a host of anti-democratic forms of exclusion. These included the exclusion of blacks, Indians, and women as full citizens; it also triggered state-directed removal policies and violence against Indians, black runaways (via the Fugitive Slave Law) and whites critical of the erection of this settlement nation. By 1851, the United States had reduced Indian Territory to parcels of land in what would become Oklahoma through the Indian Reservations Act. Coming 25 years after Cooper's publication of *The Last of the Mohicans* – a novel whose title is evocative of, if not readily associated with, genocide – it was a fulfillment of Jefferson's "democratic" vision. Indeed, the American reservation system made plausible the idea that Native Americans would no longer be a visible part of civic life for anyone east of the Mississippi River, and perhaps anywhere else.

Indian removal, chattel slavery, and the perpetuation of female domesticity were all interlocking features of American westward settlement. Those voices in opposition, including that of Ralph Waldo Emerson, were unable to overcome the torrent of popular support for expansion. Nevertheless, Emerson argued in an 1838 letter to President Martin Van Buren:

> You, sir, will bring down that renowned chair in which you sit into infamy if your seal is set to this instrument of perfidy; and the name of this nation, hitherto the sweet omen of religion and liberty, will stink to the world.
>
> (Emerson, 29, 2004)

Emerson was one voice among the Transcendentalist movement to also vehemently oppose war with Mexico. Other writers were more oblique in their criticism, including Nathaniel Hawthorne, who elected to revisit white brutality against Indians in the context of his stories, including New England's founding.

While women's suffrage would make many of its initial gains in the western states in the second half of the nineteenth century, those political gains would not be advanced at the federal level; nor would many of those rights later conferred be achieved in other areas, including education, property, and status within families. With a few notable exceptions beyond Harriet Beecher Stowe, the success of "damned scribbling women" – Hawthorne's flippant remark about the increased presence of women authors in America – was a late-century phenomenon. Nevertheless, feminist works began to dot the literary landscape, though few of these would attend to life beyond the gaze of white, middle-, and upper-class women.

Tiffany K. Wayne has pointed out that the contributions of women to the Transcendentalist movement and American intellectual history were far greater than is often depicted (Wayne, 2005). Given that Transcendental thought emphasized the uniqueness of each individual in society, women thinkers and writers began with the arduous task of arguing for the individuality of women beyond their social function as wives and mothers, while at the same time engaging the broader philosophical questions of how reasoning members of society could at once belong to a state while ethically remaining apart from its political acts found to be antithetical to one's conscience.

This intellectual independence ran counter to the government's focus upon women, particularly white women, as maintainers of racial purity in western settlements, and their attendant role as guardians of civilization within the home (Frymer, 279). Westward expansion meant establishing Anglo culture in formerly native, Catholic, and Spanish territories, a challenge to prevailing notions of what constituted the best of the nation's racial and cultural stock. Ironically, reordering the geographical and political landscape of the nation along western lines meant returning to older, and more rooted, notions of community, even as those communities were shaken by the new migration. Even the expansion of women's suffrage in western states like Wyoming carried an imperative of continuing the preferred racial order, as the lure of voting rights was offered to incentivize the settlement of white women in the western territories, thus staving off the possibility (likelihood) of interracial mixing.[10] Such policies were part of a global, European colonial strategy (Jacobs, 22, 2009).

The anthropologist Ann L. Stoler dubbed this new reality "the intimacies of empire," the programmatic design of race and gender's interplay in creating white settler societies (Stoler, 2010). In this light, female domesticity is at once passive in relegating women to the home while at the same time politically assertive, in that women were to play an active role in socially policing the sexual desires of white men (even as theirs were policed). American political thought, with rare exception, has not sufficiently examined the intellectual traditions of liberalism, as well as Christian thought, in excavating the socio-sexual dynamics of western expansion – the defining event of America's economic and political transformation.

In speaking of the "Mexicanization of American politics" (an expression thankfully nearly out of vogue), historians and political scientists in the past have expressed a kind of gratitude for the nation's having avoided the type of political instability that has episodically racked Mexico. But this expression also contains a separate seed of thought: namely, that Mexico's chaotic politics is in some ways owing to its mixed racial and cultural heritage: one that speaks to the perpetual need to guard against debasing incursions into the foremost of Anglo institutions – the family.

As Jill Lepore and others have pointed out, the Spanish "other" was an instrumental creation in establishing social and cultural parameters around the concept of "Englishness" (Lepore, 1999). Likewise, in building an American empire, new social parameters were essential in erecting (or more properly, transferring) a preferred hierarchy into western territories. That this empire was in fact created at all is perhaps more astonishing than the use of the old intellectual and political tools to build it. Much was betrayed in the exchange.

Conclusion

The components of the Compromise of 1850 are less familiar today than those found in the Missouri Compromise of 1820, but they are no less important to understanding the growth of American empire. Vast tracts of land that would later make up whole or parts of the states of New Mexico, Utah, Nevada, and Arizona would, upon being granted statehood, decide whether or not they wished to remain free or become slave states. This notion of popular sovereignty, embedded within the idea that democracy could in fact be enacted to deny basic freedom to others, however counterintuitive, made great sense when viewed through the lens of republican expansion as racially contingent. Democracy and liberty had been for whites; it may, or may not be, depending on the political circumstances, for others.

But the Compromise went even further, stipulating that the Fugitive Slave Act was to be enforced by requiring citizens of free states to assist in the return of enslaved blacks who had made it into free territory. Such "fugitives" were also to be denied a trial by jury, further rendering a legal system already tilted against racial justice a tool of racial oppression. While California was admitted into the Union as a free state, the nation's capital, Washington, DC, was allowed to continue slavery while being compelled to no longer engage in its trade. The public face of democracy was to be kept as unblemished as possible, however increasingly difficult this had become.

These were the fruits of the Louisiana Purchase, western expansion, settlement, and the agreement to allow slavery into those territories where it had not previously been. This was Lincoln's lawyerly argument against war with Mexico, and its predictable aftermath. Four years later, in the aftermath of another compromise – the Kansas-Nebraska Act, which ended restrictions against slavery above the 36° 30' line established by the Missouri Compromise – Lincoln would reject the notion of popular sovereignty. "Our republican robe is soiled," he said, "and trailed in the dust. Let us repurify it" (McPherson, 127, 1991).

Unlike the radical abolitionists who had presumed the Constitution itself to be a compromise with evil, Lincoln thought it a sufficient conduit to channel more radical notions of liberty – read mainly through the Declaration of Independence's commitment to human equality. He would not accept Chief Justice Roger B. Taney's claim that the Constitution "was formed on the white basis." The truth is, it had been so formed, and it was that fact that drove the better part of national political development in the nineteenth century. While Taney's decision in *Dred Scott* was widely condemned as a scourge upon the best sentiments of American democracy at the time, the failure, both then and now, is to reconcile the historical record supporting Taney's understanding of the founding with progressive political and social movements to redirect the nation's republican identity. It is not only possible to believe Taney and Lincoln to be both right – it is essential to dispensing with the mythology of American exceptionalism, including one of its grandest myths: the nation's growth as an "Empire of Liberty."

The early political history of America was one of striking and intermittent re-orderings of the national political character. Moving from the

Articles of Confederation to a federal republic with a powerful executive (1777–1787), a party-based democratic republic aspiring to a revolution of small, local representative governments gave way to the vision of a large, powerful state whose expanse was of questionable ability for republican virtue to tame; and then, an Empire of Liberty descended by degrees to one of conquest (1819–1848), racial internment (1830–1890), and creeping universal slavery (1830, 1850, 1854).

Like the story of the self-deluded protagonist in Nathaniel Hawthorne's "Young Goodman Brown," the pace of American political development did not allow for self-reflection. For Brown, it was an "unconscious walk" into a dark abyss of sin – one filled with what Brown imagined to be grave dangers and evils – including the specter of "blood thirsty Indians." But Hawthorne knew better than to let Brown – and his readers of this classic 1835 short story – off so easily. It was Brown, after all, who in this tale of innocence lost "was himself the chief horror of the scene" (Hawthorne, 119, 1987).

Notes

1. Thomas Jefferson, Letter to John Holmes, April 22, 1820. Library of Congress, Washington, DC. www.loc.gov/exhibits/jefferson/159.html.
2. Ibid.
3. Washington Farewell Address, The Papers of George Washington, University of Virginia. http://gwpapers.virginia.edu/documents_gw/farewell/transcript.html.
4. Thomas Jefferson, First Inaugural Address, The Papers of Thomas Jefferson, Princeton University Press. https://jeffersonpapers.princeton.edu/selected-documents/first-inaugural-address-0.
5. Theodore J. Lowi, "Bend Sinister: How the Constitution Saved the Republic and Lost Itself: The 2008 James Madison Lecture," *PS: Political Science and Politics*, 42(1), 3–9, 2009.
6. Emerson had been slow in moving towards the abolitionist movement, but he became an impassioned opponent of slavery once there. See Louis Menand, *The Metaphysical Club: A Story of Ideas in America* (New York: Farrar, Straus, and Giroux, 2001), 20–22.
7. https://liberalarts.utexas.edu/coretexts/_files/resources/texts/1848Declarationof Sentiments.pdf.
8. Justice Harlan's dissent in *Plessy v. Ferguson* (1896), for example, makes the case for racial integration for blacks by noting how the "despised Chinese" are afforded this right.

9. See Claire Jean Kim, "The Racial Triangulation of Asian Americans," *Politics and Society*, 27(1), 105–138, 1999.
10. "Women's suffrage was meant to increase the number of women coming west and give a greater vote to the stable parts of the community." See Garry Wills, *A Necessary Evil: A History of American Distrust of Government* (New York: Simon & Schuster, 1999), 339.

References

Valerie Babb, *Whiteness Visible: The Meaning of Whiteness on American Literature and Culture* (New York: New York University Press, 1998).

Brigette Bailey, Katheryn P. Viens, and Conrad Edick White (Eds.), *Margaret Fuller and Her Circles* (Durham, NH: University of New Hampshire Press, 2013).

John C. Calhoun, *The Works of John C. Calhoun*, Vol. 2 (Loschberg, Germany: Jazzybee Verlag, 2017).

James Fenimore Cooper, *The Last of the Mohicans* (New York: Empire Books, 2011).

Frederick Douglass, *Frederick Douglass, Selected Speeches and Writings* (Philip S. Foner, Ed.) (Chicago, IL: Lawrence Hill Books, 1999).

Ralph Waldo Emerson, *The Political Emerson: Essential Writings on Politics and Social Reform* (David M. Robinson, Ed.) (Boston, MA: Beacon Press, 2004).

Eric Foner, *The Fiery Trial: Abraham Lincoln and American Slavery* (New York: W.W. Norton, 2010).

Paul Frymer, *Building an American Empire: The Era of Territorial and Political Expansion* (Princeton, NJ: Princeton University Press, 2017).

Leslie F. Goldstein, *The US Supreme Court and Racial Minorities: Two Centuries of Judicial Review on Trial* (Northampton, MA: Edward Elgar, 2017).

Mitchell K. Hall, *Opposition to War: An Encyclopedia of US Peace and Antiwar Movements* (Santa Barbara, CA: ABC-CLIO, 2018).

Nathaniel Hawthorne, *Young Goodman Brown and Other Tales* (Brian Harding, Ed.) (Oxford, UK: Oxford University Press, 1987).

Harold Holzer, *Lincoln at Cooper Union: The Speech that Made Abraham Lincoln President* (New York: Simon and Schuster, 2004).

Margaret Jacobs, *White Mother to a Dark Race: Settler Colonialism, Maternalism, and the Removal of Indigenous Children in the American West and Australia, 1880–1940* (Omaha, NB: University of Nebraska, 2009).

S.T. Joshi, *Documents in American Prejudice: An Anthology of Writings on Race from Thomas Jefferson to David Duke* (New York: Basic Books, 1999).

Arthur Kaledin, *Tocqueville and His America: A Darker Horizon* (New Haven, CT: Yale University Press, 2011).

Ibram X. Kendi, *Stamped from the Beginning: The Definitive History of Racist Ideas in America* (New York: Nation Books, 2016).

Roger G. Kennedy, *Mr. Jefferson's Lost Cause: Land, Farmers, Slavery, and the Louisiana Purchase* (New York: Oxford University Press, 2003).

Linda Kerber, *Women of the Republic: Intellect and Ideology in Revolutionary America* (Chapel Hill, NC: University of North Carolina Press, 1997).

Claire Jean Kim, "The Racial Triangulation of Asian Americans," *Politics and Society*, 27(1), 105–138, 1999.

Jill Lepore, *In the Name of War: King Philip's War and the Origins of American Identity* (New York: Vintage Books, 1999).

Jan Ellen Lewis and Peter S. Onuf (Eds.), *Sally Hemings and Thomas Jefferson: History, Memory, and Civic Culture* (Charlottesville, VA: University of Virginia Press, 1999).

Theodore J. Lowi, "Bend Sinister: How the Constitution Saved the Republic and Lost Itself: The 2008 James Madison Lecture," *PS: Political Science and Politics*, 42(1), 3–9, 2009.

James McPherson, *Abraham Lincoln and the Second American Revolution* (New York: Oxford University Press, 1991).

Herman Melville, *Moby-Dick* (Berkeley, CA: Arion Press, 1979).

Louis Menand, *The Metaphysical Club: A Story of Ideas in America* (New York: Farrar, Straus, and Giroux, 2001).

Ann Stoler, *Carnal Knowledge and Imperial Power: Race and the Intimate in Colonial Rule* (Berkeley, CA: University of California Press, 2010).

Alexis de Tocqueville, *Democracy in America* (Harvey Mansfield and Delba Winthrop, Eds.) (Chicago, IL: University of Chicago, 2000).

Alexis de Tocqueville, *Democracy in America and Two Essays on America* (New York: Penguin Books, 2013).

Tiffany K. Wayne, *Woman Thinking: Feminism and Transcendentalism in Nineteenth- Century America* (Lanham, MD: Lexington Books, 2005).

Garry Wills, *A Necessary Evil: A History of American Distrust of Government* (New York: Simon & Schuster, 1999).

Garry Wills, *Negro President: Jefferson and the Slave Power* (New York: Houghton Mifflin, 2003).

David Wooten, *The Essential Federalist and Anti-Federalist Papers* (Seattle, WA: Pacific Publishing Studio, 2003).

CHAPTER FOUR
FRACTURE AND REUNION: 1850–1877

Introduction

The Irish-born reporter William Russell of the *London Times* may have been the first person to write about American exceptionalism with irony. Interested in tracking how foreign governments were reporting the early months of the Civil War, the *New York Times* ran a column on Russell's observations. On September 4, 1861, it was reported that Russell had written:

> There is one thing about civil wars, they do not last long. It is probable that the "exceptionalism," if one may use the word, on which the Americans rather pride themselves, will not prevail in the case of the struggle between North and South.[1]

Of course, Russell was proven wrong – the American Civil War did last long – attesting to American exceptionalism's veracity, at least in this regard.

The American experiment with representative government was flagging at mid-century, and while the very idea of republicanism was the basis for notions of American exceptionalism, its demise could be witnessed within the lifetime of an individual. The durability of American democracy was a question from the very beginning. As early as 1838, Abraham Lincoln spoke to the subject during a speech in Springfield, Illinois:

> At what point shall we expect the approach of danger? By what means shall we fortify against it? Shall we expect some transatlantic military giant, to step the Ocean and crush us at a blow? Never! ... If destruction be our lot, we must ourselves be its author and finisher. As a nation of freemen, we must live through all time, or die by suicide.
>
> (Lincoln, in Gienapp, 10, 2002)

As the historian Eric Foner has pointed out, free labor was the cornerstone of the Republican Party's political philosophy before 1860 (Foner, 12, 1995). The Civil War historian and Lincoln biographer James McPherson even drew psychological ties to Lincoln's childhood relationship with his father – one in which Lincoln was forced to work brutally hard clearing land, and without pay – to help explain Lincoln's opposition to slavery's expansion (McPherson, 3, 2009). The politics of labor was indeed contentious, as southerners overwhelmingly viewed enslaved blacks as property, and therefore outside the bounds of natural law as applied to human beings, let alone citizens. The Republican Party, not fully representative of northern political sentiments, nevertheless widely supported the notion that labor should be free, and that slavery was the antithesis to both biblical and humanistic injunctions against the institution.

Perhaps the greatest unattended to question dating to the Constitutional Convention was which quality of a nation self-described as a commercial republic would (or should) predominate – commerce or self-government? Alexander Hamilton's fixation on America becoming a commercial republic was one that preferably did not include slavery. Nevertheless, neither Hamilton nor any of the nation's founders saw fit to make the issue greater in importance than union. Hence, the organizing principle of the nation would be representative government, with a commercial aspect its modality. This could only be made possible by countenancing racial hierarchy and chattel slavery. Few, if any, asked whether or not representative government and capitalism were difficult partners. The early abolitionist movement did raise this concern, although, more often than not, anti-slavery arguments were tied to moral claims rooted in religion (Huebner, 45, 2016).

These religious arguments were often powerful broadsides against the evident hypocrisy slavery evinced in a nation whose chief distinctiveness was said to be rooted in liberty. As the influential free black thinker and businessman James Forten wrote in 1813:

> We hold this truth to be self evident that God created all men equal is one of the most prominent features of the Declaration of Independence, and in that glorious fabric of collected wisdom, our noble Constitution. This idea embraces the Indian and the European, the savage and the Saint, the Peruvian and the Laplander, the white man and the African, and whatever measures are adopted subversive of this estimable privilege, are in direct violation of the letter and spirit of the out Constitution.
>
> (Huebner, 48)

Herman Melville would fill his ship the *Pequod* with such diverse members of humanity, imagining a kind of state at sea, subject to not only the natural forces of wind and storm, but those internal ones underlying human consciousness. The American ship, such as it was (and is), could not be imagined outside of the context of its deepest contradiction – and that could only be made plausible by mirroring the pigmentocracy of the nation and its history. As the writer and literary critic Harold Bloom has recently written: "My students find in the *Pequod*'s crew a prophecy of the newer America breaking upon us now, to the perplexity of the wretched theocrats, plutocrats, and aging moralists" (Bloom, 135, 2015).

Of course, the progressive forces of America have always imagined an "aging" and ultimately passing, cohort of intolerant and bigoted countryman. The optimism of Bloom's students belies a perhaps more disturbing phenomenon: Somehow the theocrats, plutocrats, and moralists are perennially replicated in America. In this way, *Moby-Dick* is less prophecy, and more of a work of science fiction, a journey into the surreal, where each generation must repeat the failings of the *Pequod* and its assent to Ahab's madness.

American political thought has had to wrestle with the fact that the nation's historic compromises have been successes in only the most sanguine reading of its past. This chapter confronts two of those compromises which bookend the horrors and redemptive qualities of the Civil War: the Compromise of 1850, and its less studied counterpart, the Compromise of 1877. Each tragic – one for its postponement of racial justice, the other for its retreat from it – they speak to how republican forms can be woefully insufficient bulwarks against the conceits of power and willful moral negligence. War with Mexico, a domestic war in Kansas, and a war of ideas fought over the compatibility of white supremacy with self-government (in the *Dred Scott* case and in the Lincoln–Douglas debates) define the period as much as the Civil War does. That latter disaster, one unequaled in American history, was laid upon the ashes of smaller, but inciting ones. And these were all premised upon the failings of the great commercial republican dream. The ends of capital, unfettered as they were, pressed towards man as property; the aspirations of democratic life could not contend with them for very long.

In considering Abraham Lincoln, the age's best and most contemplative voice on democracy emanating from within the political system, it is worth noting his shift towards radical political thought. This should not be mistaken for radical politics – something quite different. Lincoln's Gettysburg Address and Second Inaugural were master works in political thought – his Ten Per Cent Plan and moderate vision of reconstruction, the artful compromises of a master statesman. Lincoln's greatest gift to his republic was a vision beyond what the founders had bequeathed to their heirs. Yet somehow, magically, Lincoln managed to reimagine their legacy along lines of his choosing. That the more genteel, and indeed more elegiac, address at Gettysburg has become America's national poem can be attributed to the fact that the Second Inaugural, clunkier and less musical, asks much more of its citizens. It makes demands upon the heart and conscience that remain unfulfilled.

Compromise, Sovereignty, and the Politics of Race

> The very best thing that could possibly be done towards the abolition of Slavery would be for the North to stop talking about it. Ten years of absolute silence would do more than fifty of turmoil and hostility, toward a peaceful removal of the evil.[2]

This was the conclusion of the *New York Times* in early 1859. Reflecting the conservative Republican thought of the period, the *Times* preferred the quiescence found in union rather than the volatile uncertainty a frontal assault upon slavery would likely bring (Foner, 188, 1995). The silencing of anti-slavery voices had long been the basis for compromise at the Constitutional Convention, and most famously, in Congress, over the years.

What was new by the middle of the nineteenth century was the expansion of slavery west – first through the annexation and subsequent statehood of Texas, then through the acquisition of nearly half of Mexico's territory through war. This expansion, more than anything else, transformed the United States into an empire. Lincoln had opposed annexation on the grounds of his opposition to slavery's expansion. He also deemed it contrary to the principle of the separation of powers central to the Constitution. In an 1848 letter to his law partner William Herndon, Lincoln wrote:

> Allow the President to invade a neighboring nation, whenever *he* shall deem it necessary to repel an invasion, and you allow him to do so, *whenever he may choose to say* he deems it necessary for such purpose – and you allow him to make war at pleasure.
>
> (Gienapp, 20; italics in original)

Executive power was first fused with a populist, ostensibly democratic politics, under Andrew Jackson. It continued under President James K. Polk, with Whig opposition reflecting a minority view within the country. National power and the right to unfettered expansion ("manifest destiny") would later become a hallmark of progressivism, showing democracy's cozy relationship with imperial projects. That such expansion of executive and national power were directed against indigenous peoples and nonwhite polities underscores the dearth of countervailing ideas to white supremacy present in American political thought. The Compromise of 1850 allowed for slavery's expansion through the most "democratic" of means – popular sovereignty. Should states emergent from newly admitted territories to the Union wish to allow slavery, they could, subject to a vote reflective of the "will of the people." Treaties with Indian tribes, popular sovereignty, and legislative compromise were all constitutionally sanctioned forms of racial oppression – acts that conferred legitimacy upon the racial hierarchy embedded in American life. The supposed genius of the American political system for compromise was one rooted in the acceptability of white supremacy. Aside from this feature – endemic to the Compromises of 1820, 1850, and 1877 – was the otherwise ordinary bargaining for political and economic rights to regional interests (Farber, 9, 2003).

Louis Hartz came to a very different interpretation of this history in his classic work *The Liberal Tradition in America*. Hartz wrote:

> The political thought of the Civil War symbolizes not the weakness of the American liberal idea but its strength, its vitality, and its utter dominion over the American mind. The strange agonies the Southerners endured trying to break out of the grip of Locke and the way the nation greeted their effort, stand as a permanent testimony to the power of the idea.
>
> (Hartz, 177, 1991)

Relegating the Civil War to a crisis with Lockean liberalism (and the inevitable defeat of southern opposition) is precisely the kind of thinking Lincoln attacks in his Second Inaugural. The point is that the South was not out of step with Lockean liberalism; Lockean liberalism was out of step with racial egalitarianism and black personhood. This was not merely a struggle over regional political thought, and Lincoln understood that in a post-slavery America, such thinking would be as dangerous to the democratic project of a nation truly "conceived in liberty" as the one that compromised on the question of black humanity.

The source of that dimension of American political thought was in a word, capitalism. As Eric Foner has written, "It was well known that in the major cities of the East the wealthiest citizens placed the preservation of the Union (and of their markets and business connections in the South) above agitation of the slavery question" (Foner, 21, 1995). The American liberal tradition was compatible with white supremacy – and the politics of popular sovereignty underscored the vitality of the relationship. The Missouri Compromise of 1820, rooted in practical economic and political power dynamics, was reflective of the most consistent and enduring part of the American ethos – managing the complexities of economic gain and expansion. Race has had much to do with the nature of those complexities, and in the aftermath of war with Mexico, the Speaker of the House, Henry Clay, once again, returned to the essentials of white self-government in crafting the Compromise of 1850. In the end, the United States brought California into the Union, a territory President James Buchanan described as "composed chiefly of our own kindred, of a people speaking our own language, and educated for self-government under our own institutions" (Frymer, 200, 2017). It was a familiar argument, dating as far back as Washington's Farewell Address, where the outgoing president reiterated the premise of national unity – ethno-political homogeneity.

"You are saved," cried Captain Delano, Herman Melville's protagonist in his fictionalized account of a slave revolt aboard a Spanish ship. "You are saved: what has cast such a shadow upon you?" Captain Delano's response, offered without explanation, is simply, "The Negro." The passage in the novella *Benito Cereno*, later to become an epigraph to Ralph Ellison's novel *Invisible Man*, haunts because Melville understood that even in victory, the underlying and faulty premise of white supremacy offered tenuous psychological cover for those insistent upon its durability. That "shadow" was a dark reminder of the nation's inability to resolve the tension between slavery and liberty; for Melville, writing in 1855, it seemed to be a problem to be passed on to some unknown future generation to address. When Captain Delano encounters an enslaved African engaged in tying a knot on the deck of the ship, we can see Melville's insight into this mystifying arrangement:

> Captain Delano crossed over to him and stood in silence surveying the knot, his mind, by a not uncongenial transition, passing from its own entanglements to those of the hemp. For intricacy, such a knot he had never seen in an American ship, nor indeed in any other. The old man looked like an Egyptian priest making Gordian knots for the temple of Ammon. The knot seemed a combination of double-bowline-knot, treble-crown-knot, back-handed-well-knot, knot-in-and-out-knot, and jamming knot.
>
> At last, puzzled to comprehend the meaning of such a knot, Captain Delano addressed the knotter: "What are you knotting there, my man?"
>
> "The knot," was the brief reply, without looking up.
>
> "So it seems; but what is it for?"
>
> "For someone else to undo," muttered back the old man, plying his fingers harder than ever, the knot being now nearly completed.
>
> (Melville, 89, 1986)

From Washington to Lincoln, the "knot" persisted, passed on from one generation to the next. Like the mythical Gordian knot, it could only be undone by cutting, and with horrific consequences at that. All compromises with the institution of slavery only further tightened the knot, and at mid-century, Melville, most astute on the power of race in American life, understood the intractable nature of the problem. The end of the feasibility of compromise came in 1857 with the *Dred Scott* decision.

In *Scott v. Sanford* (1857), Chief Justice Roger B. Taney ruled that blacks were "of an inferior order and altogether unfit to associate with the white race" (Foner, 93, 2010). Practically, this meant that both free and enslaved blacks could not be guaranteed freedom even in states and territories where slavery had been prohibited. The caste system in America, regionalized, contested, and a source of embarrassment, had become nationalized and sanctioned by the highest court in the land. As Eric Foner (Foner, 93, 2010) has noted, Taney's decision superseded the argument for popular sovereignty, in effect claiming that even if whites voted in opposition to slavery, their very whiteness amounted to a power greater than that of a democratic vote when it came to the ability to possess black people. White supremacy was now not only the law of the land – it was a fact greater than the idea of self-government itself.

As Garry Wills has argued:

> Lincoln was able to achieve the loftiness, ideality, and brevity of the Gettysburg Address because he had spent a good part of the 1850s repeatedly relating all the most sensitive issues of the day to the Declaration's supreme principle. If all men are created equal, they cannot be property.
>
> (Wills, 120, 1992)

Taney, invoking the same document and history, reached an altogether different conclusion:

> It is difficult at this day to realize the state of public opinion in relation to that unfortunate race which prevailed in the civilized and enlightened portions of the world at the time of the Declaration of Independence and when the Constitution of the United States was framed and adopted. But the public history of every European nation displays it in a manner too plain to be mistaken.

They had for more than a century before been regarded as beings of an inferior order, and altogether unfit to associate with the white race either in social or political relations, and so far inferior that they had no rights which the white man was bound to respect, and that the negro might justly and lawfully be reduced to slavery for his benefit.[3]

Where Lincoln viewed the Framers of the Constitution (and Jefferson) as having accepted slavery's position as a constitutional right, it was one that was marked out for limitation, and ultimately, extinction. Taney's history may have been far closer to reality, but Lincoln's interpretation was aspirational. The distance between Taney and Lincoln, however great on the question of slavery as presented in the *Dred Scott* decision, reflected a far closer and recurring divide historically. America was a land of liberty where liberty was restricted. That liberty was based on racial essentialism. As Michael Hanchard has written, it was a phenomenon dating as far back as the Greek polis, where democratic citizenship long excluded slaves, foreigners, and women (Hanchard, 2018).

That the solution to the divide between Lincoln and Taney was resolved over the course of a four-year war costing 620,000 lives speaks to the shortcomings of American political thought on the question of race, and as fundamentally, the meaning of democracy. Lincoln gambled his political career in 1858 on his ability to make the claim that white supremacy, democracy, and the restriction of slavery's expansion could exist in the same nation. Lincoln would lose that gamble, forcing a more fundamental break with slavery's persistence in a nation whose founding documents were committed to citizenship rooted in assent, rather than blood.

According to his biographer, Brenda Wineapple, Nathaniel Hawthorne, like many white northerners, opposed slavery while subscribing to white superiority and the social exclusion of blacks. "What about slavery? And why doesn't he [Hawthorne] write about it?" wrote Mary Mann to her friend Sophia, Hawthorne's wife (Wineapple, 328, 2003). The truth was that Hawthorne straddled a cautionary middle ground, not unfamiliar political terrain to Abraham Lincoln, who in 1858 was seeking a seat in the United States Senate. "The good of others, like our own happiness, is not to be attained by direct effort, but incidentally," Hawthorne wrote to Elizabeth Peabody in October of 1857 (Wineapple, 331). It was the kind of argument Lincoln hoped would prevail against Stephen Douglas in Illinois.

"I have no purpose to introduce political and social equality between the white and black races," Lincoln said in the first debate with Douglas (Lepore, 277, 2018):

> But I hold that, notwithstanding all this, there is no reason in the world why the negro is not entitled to all the natural rights enumerated in the Declaration of Independence, the right to life, liberty, and the pursuit of happiness.
>
> (Lepore, 278)

As Jill Lepore notes, Lincoln believed he had advanced the debate, irrespective of his centrist stand on slavery. "Though I now sink out of view, and shall be forgotten," Lincoln wrote in the aftermath of his defeat by Douglas, "I believe I have made some marks which will tell for the cause of civil liberty long after I am gone" (Lepore, 279).

Those "marks" included a robust defense of Jefferson's long view with respect to slavery's ultimate abolition; Lincoln likewise defended the core principle of black humanity – that whatever whites held to be their superior position, they were not entitled to any superior legal protection or authority under the Constitution. This was less of a legalistic argument than it was a moral one. Lincoln argued a point which would later become foundational to his theory of racial justice laid out in the Second Inaugural: blacks are ultimately a created people, and therefore entitled to all the rights conferred by a God who makes no distinctions among those he created:

> I agree with Judge Douglas he [the negro] is not my equal in many respects, but in the right to eat the bread without leave of anybody else, which his own hand earns, he is my equal, and the equal of Judge Douglas, and the equal of every living man.
>
> (McPherson, 52, 1991)

The right to "eat the bread which his own hand produces" is a biblical principle found in the book of Genesis. While it is an article of faith most associated with Lincoln's Second Inaugural, it was employed by Lincoln earlier, and was indicative of his understanding of the relationship between free labor and race. This proved to be a losing argument in Illinois, where Douglas dominated the "downstate" vote; nevertheless, it was the "progressive" ground between abolition and slavery.

Popular sovereignty, however successful politically, could not be described in those terms, given its acceptance of slavery's expansion. Lincoln's moderate position was to the left politically on the question of slavery, and a minority view among whites, even in a northern state such as Illinois. Many, like Hawthorne, preferred silence on the question, lest it produce a radical departure from the status quo.

Violence and the Limits of Liberal Politics: John Brown to the Wilderness

North America had long been a continent roiled by violence. That violence, marked by bloodshed between the indigenous peoples and the European settlers who encountered them, was enacted along racial lines. The bloody conflicts in Europe had been motivated by religion primarily, though the rise of racism wedded religion and blood – mainly through subordination, violence, and the expulsion of Europe's Jewish population (Fredrickson, 2016). In the New World, however, color became the mark of "barbarism." But national colonial efforts also led to Spanish and English conflict, and later, a French and Indian War that further delineated lines of savagery and civilization, dating back to King Philip's War.

None of these conflicts among Europeans reached the level of devastation as the American Civil War – a four-year conflict that saw 2 percent of the population become victims of its horrors (Faust, 266, 2008). Such a level of death in today's America would be the equivalent of a holocaust of over six million dead – at the hands of fellow countrymen. What kind of country could produce such bloodshed? What features of its polity – both structural and theoretical – could produce such mass carnage? What Madison and the framers of the Constitution accounted for, but could not control, was the advent of a vocal and influential abolitionist movement in the North, coupled with territorial expansion that antagonized, rather than diffused, pro- and anti-slavery forces. Underlying these differences was the question of sectional power and the type of republic the United States was to be. The formerly commercial and now emerging industrial nation America had become threatened southern economic and political power. The ability to evenly distribute this power was forever altered by the Court's ruling in *Dred Scott.* John Brown then lit the match that brought the inevitable conflagration to life.

"Before the Civil War, no one, except John Brown, could conceive of a way to end slavery without the consent of slaveowners," Eric Foner has written. "[T]here was simply no constitutional way that this could be accomplished" (Foner, 125, 2010). By 1859, Brown had already murdered five white men in Kansas suspected of being slaveholders. His militancy was but one sign of the growing violence not only in Kansas, where a war was afoot to determine liberty's outcome in the state, but in the rest of the nation as well. Nevertheless, Brown's 1859 plot to incite a slave rebellion through an attempted siege at Harpers Ferry rekindled southern rationales for the need for federal protection of their constitutional rights – namely the right to "property," that Brown and other radical abolitionists threatened. In addition, Brown's act sparked the rise of militias in the South and placed the nation on a near war footing.

While Frederick Douglass admired the tenacity of Brown, he opposed his foolhardy move at Harpers Ferry; Nathaniel Hawthorne, true to form, said "Nobody was ever more justly hanged" (Wineapple, 333). What made Brown's actions unique was that the inherently violent system of slavery – one that sanctioned violence against fugitive slaves and their benefactors – was under assault by the violence of a northern white man – someone hoping to incite a slave insurrection. "Threats of secession, if [southern] demands were not met, became increasingly common" (Farber, 11). "Bleeding Kansas," the caning of Charles Sumner, and other violent acts, including Brown's raid, all raised the stakes, serving notice that there was a breakdown in the nation's constitutional system, one that had been premised on not only checks and balances, and a separation of powers; it had also been based on the indefinite silence of slavery's opponents. That arrangement had now come to an end.

The abolitionist movement and women's suffrage movement had helped bring the question of slavery to a head. "The house divided" that Lincoln invoked in a speech in Springfield, Illinois in

1858 presupposed a certain uniformity of opinion among those opposed to slavery. While southern white women such as Mary Chestnut have been the focus of much attention from historians for their literary value in capturing pro-slavery doctrine in the South, northern white women's views have been less scrutinized. An excellent counter to this trend is Brenda Wineapple's biography of Nathaniel Hawthorne, which captures the "unexceptional" racism of his wife, Sophia (Wineapple, 329). In a letter to Elizabeth Peabody, written in the aftermath of Taney's ruling in the *Dred Scott* case, Sophia wrote:

> You surely must know that there are advocates of amalgamation, & also that there are abolitionists who uphold that the black race is virtually equal to the white …. I did not suppose *you* did either, and I was wondering how *anyone* could.
>
> (Wineapple, 329)

Opposition to slavery in the North was hardly a given. "In New England itself, the rural areas and small towns were the most radical," Eric Foner has recorded. "The cities, with their commercial ties to the South and large numbers of immigrants, tended to be more conservative" (Foner, 107, 1995). The cosmopolitanism of the urban elite in the North did not mitigate against racist attitudes – even among white women; perhaps especially so. It is a difficult and troubling historical question to measure, but the advantages of white privilege offset those lost to patriarchy – at least for some. Indeed, as Michael Hanchard reminds us, "As in many instances of social conflict described as 'racial,' gendered dynamics are embedded within so-called racial or racist dynamics" (Hanchard, 130). That these dynamics vacillate between progressive and racialist theories suggests all the more need to more deeply analyze their history – particularly in the American North, where presumptions of anti-slavery (and anti-racist) antagonisms often defy the historical record.

This phenomenon played out in the history of western expansion as well. It was in the American West where women's voting rights first began to flourish (Wills, 1992). The irony of that democratic accomplishment is that it was attended by, and arguably made plausible by, the extension of slavery and Indian Removal. As Paul Frymer has written:

[T]o the degree that women were discussed in these debates, [over western expansion] they were typically deemed essential for the success of national settlement efforts because permanent settlement meant the establishment of families. Women were necessary to make sure these families were not just conquerors but civilizers and domesticators .... White women were also frequently seen as necessary to make sure that white men did not stray; in frontier lands where white women were few, there was ongoing concern in Washington that the nation's racial orders maintained stability.

(Frymer, 279)

To this point, women had the right to vote in all states but one (New Mexico) west of the Rockies by 1914 (Wills, 339–340, n21, 2002).

Slavery could not have lasted for centuries in America without this kind of political exchange and social deal-making. The historian Rebecca Edwards may have put it best:

[It] is not that the parties battled over the family instead of slavery, industrialization, or other crucial issues. Rather, it is that all these concerns were intertwined, and a particular model of family life was central to each party's larger world view.

(Edwards, 176, 2003)

That family life was premised on the rejection of miscegenation, and the subordination of women.

These arrangements, as embedded as they were in American life, could not preclude the violent outbreak of war in 1861. In a letter written nearly one year before Robert E. Lee's surrender at Appomattox Court House, Lincoln wrote: "I claim not to have controlled events, but confess plainly that events have controlled me" (Donald, 15, 1995). Lincoln's decision to supply the federal troops at Fort Sumter in April of 1861 may not have provoked the war, but it led to Confederate President Jefferson Davis's decision to fire upon the fort, effectively beginning the Civil War. Adam Gopnik has written that Lincoln's underlying rationale for the war was reason – the need for the principles of republicanism (made stronger through Union) to prevail over secession and violence.[4]

Lincoln's fatalism may have created psychological distance between his actions and the violence that years of war had wrought. We can never know – but Lincoln's advocacy for Union above all else was the preeminent and driving force of his politics before and during the war. Indeed, Paul Frymer's analysis of Lincoln's political thought in crafting the Emancipation Proclamation shows that it was closely linked with colonization, not black equality in the United States. "You and we are different races," Lincoln told a group of black leaders meeting in Washington, DC in August of 1862. "We have between us a broader difference than exists between almost any other two races. Whether it is right or wrong I need not discuss, but this physical difference is a great disadvantage to us both" (Frymer, 248).

Lincoln's appeal for the colonization of blacks upon emancipation underscored the underlying tension – indeed antagonism – between self-government in the United States, and black personhood and racial equality. Only the magnitude of the Civil War could rearrange the relationship between liberty and race in America. After touring the battlefields of Virginia after the awesome devastation witnessed during the Wilderness Campaign, Herman Melville would write that the war brought about "an upheaval affecting the basis of things" (Faust, 201).

Melville's visit to Virginia included a meeting with General Ulysses S. Grant, whose unrelenting and bloody Wilderness campaign earned him some of the harshest criticism of the war. That Grant became a "butcher" in the face of an enemy equally tenacious in both killing and dying to preserve the institution of slavery helps explain the reasons why racial justice in America had been such an intractable dilemma for the Founders and their heirs. Melville perhaps said it best in a poem he wrote in 1864 for *Battle-Pieces and Aspects of the War*, published in 1866. The most haunting stanza of "The Armies of the Wilderness" reads:

> Did the Fathers feel mistrust?
> Can no final good be wrought?
> Over and over, again and again
> Must the fight for the Right be fought?[5]

"From the Earth," and "All Nations": Lincoln as Mystic

In 1952, Josephine Cobb, working as the chief of the Still Photo section at the National Archives, discovered what was then believed to be the first and only photograph of Abraham Lincoln at Gettysburg.[6] Lincoln's bare head can be seen amid the crowd only when greatly magnified. The image is reminiscent of similar photographs in their power to prove the miracle of some nearly fabled historical event. Babe Ruth's pointing to centerfield before homering in the 1932 World Series in Chicago comes to mind. The photograph confirms that the thing in question happened.

The photos of Lincoln and Ruth are both opaque enough to conjure the requisite credibility of the act while affirming its magic. What did Lincoln say at Gettysburg that brought ordinary speech to the realm of the mystical? Many historians have addressed this question, Garry Wills chief among them (Wills, 1992). Little more needs be said, save only that which concerns Gettysburg's relationship to the Second Inaugural – and more importantly, to the question of Lincoln's return to the theme of national redemption. What was left to be said about the purpose of the war after Gettysburg? When presented in this way, the Gettysburg Address reads like a parental encouragement – it is the light of optimism presented at a dark moment. The Second Inaugural – darker, somewhat less optimistic, is the strong medicine given to a child in recovery. That Lincoln sought the darkness of moral truth – the pain of coming to account with the Creator – makes the Second Inaugural the last word of the Gettysburg Address – and arguably, the most profound word of introspection delivered by an American president ever.

In short, the Gettysburg Address was a response to Alexander Hamilton's question asked in the first of the *Federalist Papers*: "whether societies of men are really capable or not of establishing good government from reflection and choice, or whether they are forever destined to depend for their political constitutions on accident and force."[7] Lincoln reframed the question as a test – "whether that nation, or any nation so conceived and so dedicated, can long endure" (Gienapp, 184). Despite the hopefulness of the speech and its connection to the Declaration of Independence's affirmation of human equality, it must be said that Lincoln does not answer Madison's question in the affirmative. That we believe he did suggests something about the ability of American political thought and our attachment to American exceptionalism to occlude truths present before our very eyes.

At best, Lincoln proposed an oath:

That we here highly resolve that these dead shall not have died in vain – that this nation, under God, shall have a new birth of freedom – and that government of the people, by the people, for the people, shall not perish from the earth.

(Gienapp, 184)

This promise to link black liberty with republican government – only Haiti had done so to this point in modern times – was the key to national redemption for Lincoln. This was "the new birth of freedom" after all, a turn of phrase which presupposes that some freedoms may exist along highly restrictive lines. Some 58,000 Americans fell over three days at Gettysburg – an unfathomable level of carnage. Lincoln chose to make sense of it based upon a commitment to lead a very different kind of nation. "O, let America be America," Langston Hughes would write decades later. "The land that has never been yet."[8] This is the imagined republic of Lincoln – one that makes the Declaration truly universal – and made real in a future not yet realized.

Lincoln's vision was at once retrospective and future-oriented. That he could only propose a promise to carry on the "unfinished work" of Gettysburg's dead is a sobering reminder that great uncertainty attended the prospects for national reconciliation. Lincoln's Second Inaugural grappled with that uncertainty more forthrightly. It is nearly sacrilegious to suggest the Gettysburg Address was somehow incomplete; but if Lincoln could suggest as much about the Declaration, it is only fair that he be subject to the same treatment. Indeed, Dr. Martin Luther King, Jr. (and many others) would apply that kind of historical scrutiny over the course of the Black Freedom Struggle. Lincoln applied an addendum, if not a corrective, to his speech at Gettysburg, one more profound, and perhaps far less comforting.

The Second Inaugural Address did not confer an oath, but an interpretation. Like Gettysburg, it was concerned with the meaning and purpose of misery and death inflicted upon the nation. Lincoln went further than suggesting that the war was a test or crucible for the nation and its commitment to self-government. Perhaps because of the long wind-up to its master sequence, some of its power has been lost. Nevertheless, its significance is widely recognized. Lincoln's last, poetic lines have long been the focus of the speech:

With malice toward none; with charity for all; with firmness in the right, as God gives us to see the right, let us strive on to finish the work we are in; to bind up the nation's wounds; to care for him who shall have borne the battle, and for his widow, and to his orphan – to do all which may achieve a just, and a lasting peace, among ourselves, and with all nations.

(Gienapp, 221)

Now, with the war nearly over, "the work" is less about securing republican government (as it had been at Gettysburg in the fall of 1863), and more about healing and the restoration of peace. But it is what comes before this last pledge of forgiveness and charity that gives the Second Inaugural its deeper meaning – and elevates Lincoln beyond the realm of a statesman into something far greater.

How so? For starters, Lincoln provides the greatest six words ever uttered by an American president and perhaps any democratic leader. In stating "The Almighty has His own purposes," Lincoln offers that neither North nor South could invoke the Bible to their advantage. And he also postulates that "It may seem strange that any men should dare to ask a just God's assistance in wringing their bread from the sweat of other men's faces; but let us judge not that we be not judged" (Gienapp, 221). Here, Lincoln provides moral balm to the South – despite its violating the Old Testament admonition against depriving anyone the fruits earned from their labor. But he likewise reminds the country of the New Testament power of forgiveness. This is well enough. But it has evident political purposes. Given Lincoln's interest in reuniting the country, suggesting that the South must be forgiven for the sin of slavery is less noble than it might appear at first glance. Yet Lincoln's claim that God stands outside the realm of politics is powerful. By rejecting the claim that His will is in accordance with the will of the Nation, Lincoln refuses the temptation to place Providence at the seat of a political party or leader – even when that leader or party is on the right side of a great moral issue, as was the case with American slavery. It is a great challenge to the historian of republicanism to find another moment where God's purpose is unclaimed – particularly at a moment of victory.

Yet Lincoln goes further. National reconciliation requires something more than forgiveness. The following passage is the Seal to the Gettysburg Address, and the most momentous appeal in presidential rhetoric:

> Fondly do we hope – fervently do we pray that this mighty scourge of war may speedily pass away. Yet, if God wills that it continue, until all wealth piled by the bond-man's two-hundred and fifty years of unrequited toil shall be sunk, and until every drop of blood drawn with the lash, shall be paid by another drawn with the sword, as was said three thousand years ago, so still it must be said "the judgments of the Lord, are true and righteous altogether."
>
> (Gienapp, 221)

After four years of the bloodiest war in American history, Lincoln chooses the most painful and difficult meaning to the carnage experienced by so many.

It was earned.

The great lesson of the war was that American slavery, administered in the South, and financed in the North, required a kind of righteous justice that whites would never adjudicate for themselves. The idea that the blood of blacks had to be compensated for by the blood of whites was, and is, an astounding proposition. One can only consider Lincoln's radical view of Justice in light of more contemporary moments. Imagine President George W. Bush in the aftermath of 9/11 explaining to Americans that the death and suffering of so many was the product of America's conduct around the world. The concept of "blowback" in foreign policy comes closest – but it is the province of critical intelligence analysts and perhaps anti-war activists; it is an unimaginable perspective to be shared by an American president. Perhaps it remains unimaginable, given how seldom this part of the Second Inaugural is quoted or made the point of focus in national memorials to Lincoln and the Civil War. As Ronald C. White, Jr. writes in his great study of the Second Inaugural, "If a present-day president were to use such words, they would surely jar" (White, 158, 2005).

No president since Lincoln has called the nation to this type of painful introspection. It is what sets him apart. Presidents such as FDR and Kennedy have asked the nation to make personal sacrifices. None have done so in the context of atonement. This is what is missing, and it is Lincoln's sense of atonement that has been missing in national discussions of slavery and race since.

At Gettysburg, Lincoln lacked the kind of understanding made possible by experiencing the full arc of the Civil War. In March of 1865, the war was nearly over, and Lincoln could go beyond the question of healing and move into the larger question of atonement. In doing so, he was able to return to the theme of republicanism's global future most appropriately. At Gettysburg, Lincoln ended on this note, offering that "government of the people, by the people, for the people, shall not perish from the earth." Self-government limited to the United States was not the final objective. Presaging Woodrow Wilson, Lincoln makes democracy the great objective for the world. And in the Second Inaugural, he makes a "just and lasting peace with ourselves and all nations" the predicate for doing so. This is more Kantian – the vision of a universal and perpetual peace – than Wilsonian. But it is also biblical in the sense that suffering, redemption, and peace make up the sequence by which human beings are restored to their proper relationship with God. Despite his shortcomings and late arrival to the commitment to ending slavery, Lincoln nevertheless, in the end, became, both in language and deed, the greatest American political thinker and statesman in American history. That he remains so is as much a testament to his greatness as it is to our inability, and indeed reticence, to match his level of introspection over the ensuing century and a half.

Conclusion: Reconstruction and the Capitulation of Compromise

The political scientist Theodore Lowi called the Fourteenth Amendment a revolutionary and essential part of a new American republic.[9] The promise of the Bill of Rights was now applied nationally, and while equal protection under the law and equal citizenship were guaranteed to all African Americans born in the United States, the same was true, writ large, for all Americans. In a sense, the Amendment's ratification in 1868 undid (at least legally) the centuries of compromise related to black citizenship and personhood. And it made any State's violation of the right of citizenship unlawful. Readers of Ta-Nehisi Coates' book *We Were Eight Years in Power* may be forgiven for having mistaken the title of his work for the period between the ratification of the Fourteenth Amendment and the election of Rutherford B. Hayes in 1876 (Coates, 2017). This was certainly my initial error, for it was during that window of time when the United States government was most unequivocally on the side of black rights and empowerment. Like most American dreams where race is concerned, it came to an abrupt end.

The Civil War amendments represented a radical departure from the racial state America had long been. Lincoln's assassination stymied a more moderate path towards reconstruction. Indeed, Wendell Phillips described Lincoln's Ten Per Cent Plan for readmitting southern states back into the Union as one that "frees the slave and ignores the negro" (Foner, 36, 2014). That said, Reconstruction also ignored the Native American. The United States initiated a set of policies, beginning with the Homestead Act of 1862, that made western settlement of territories – including those formerly granted to Indians – a national priority. As Paul Frymer has written:

> Many western territories came under the authority of Union army leaders during the war, with the consequence of escalating military violence toward Native American nations and resulting in some of the most violent battles and massacres of nineteenth-century Indian removal.
>
> (Frymer, 151)

The new republic enlivened by the end of slavery and the protection of black citizenship and voting rights did not preclude the continued oppression of Native Americans and repression of women's rights. And the rights of blacks were only protected for a brief time. Women's suffrage, which had been part and parcel of the abolitionist movement, did not become the natural part of a reformed, more complete democratic republic. "Feminist leaders were left with a deep sense of betrayal" upon learning that the Fourteenth Amendment would not apply to them (Foner, 255, 2014). The decoupling of women's suffrage from abolition and black rights reflected the kind of selective advancement for groups standing outside the fullness of American democracy.

Republican administration over black political rights in the South came to an end in 1877 with the compromise over the election of 1876. Rutherford B. Hayes' controversial election to the presidency over New York Democrat Samuel J. Tilden called into question national unity unlike anything since the formal end of war in 1865. Hayes' win came through the Electoral College and the final assignment of 20 of those votes from states under Republican Party rule. Southern fury was forestalled by the restoration of white home rule in the South, and promises for federal aid for southern industrialization. Likewise, federal troops no longer played a public role in the administration of electoral politics in the South. In short, "1877 marked a decisive retreat from the idea, born during the Civil War, a powerful national state protecting the fundamental rights of American citizens" (Foner, 582, 2014).

Taking Lincoln at his word, the Compromise of 1877 was a rebuke to the sacrifices made at Gettysburg and over the course of the Civil War. The return to compromise that negated black rights, temporized over the question of women's suffrage, and enabled the eradication of Indian lands under genocidal policies was, in a sense, a form of regression towards the great American mean of history. Arthur M. Schlesinger, Jr. had written that the cycles of American history typically provided an episodic possibility for progressive policies. Reform (support for what we would identify today as liberal policies) was the exception to American exceptionalism, one rooted in a conservatism prioritizing property, whiteness, maleness, and national power (Schlesinger, 1999). The swings between liberalism and conservatism have always occupied a right-of-center field of political possibilities in the United States, given that liberalism is itself a form of centrist politics almost anywhere outside of American politics.

"A house divided against itself cannot stand," Lincoln said in 1858. "It will become all one thing, or all the other." Of course, the American state, like all others, has managed to abide the gray spaces between all one thing or all another. Admitting so requires a rejection of the bounds between Good and Evil, which date from America's Puritan origins. America has never been all free, nor its entirety the province of slavery – except in the literal sense of the legal abandonment of chattel slavery. But this can't be what Lincoln meant. The "just and lasting peace" requires a freedom and equality far greater than the accordance of mere personhood through legislation. This again is the gift of the Second Inaugural. It requires an inner feat of democratic understanding to enable the possibilities for the outward justice required for the sustenance of democratic life. That the nation was torn apart in quest for the creation of an "all or nothing" nation and failed is the story of the second half of American political history and the political thought that shaped it.

Notes

1. William Russell, "The American Correspondence of the *London Times*: Another Letter from Mr. William Russell," *New York Times,* September 4, 1861.
2. *New York Times,* January 19, 1859.
3. See Taney Opinion at: www.law.cornell.edu/supremecourt/text/60/393#writing USSC_CR_0060_0393_ZO.
4. Adam Gopnik, "Abraham Lincoln, and the Birth of Stand Your Ground," *The New Yorker,* July 18, 2013.
5. From Aaron Dean-Sheehan (Ed.), *The Civil War: The Final Year Told by Those Who Lived It* (New York: The Library of America, 2014), pp. 102–109. Originally published in Herman Melville, *Battle-Pieces and Aspects of the War* (New York: Harper & Brothers, 1866).
6. From the National Archives website: https://prologue.blogs.archives.gov/2010/11/19/rare-photo-of-lincoln-at-gettysburg/.
7. http://avalon.law.yale.edu/18th_century/fed01.asp.
8. www.poetryfoundation.org/poems/147907/let-america-be-america-again.
9. Theodore J. Lowi, "Bend Sinister: How the Constitution Saved Itself and Lost the Republic," *PS: Political Science and Politics,* 42(1), 3–9, 2009.

References

Harold Bloom, *The Daemon Knows: Literary Greatness and the American Sublime* (New York: Spiegel & Grau, 2015).
Ta-Nehisi Coates, *We Were Eight Years in Power: An American Tragedy* (New York: One World Books, 2017).
Aaron Dean-Sheehan (Ed.), *The Civil War: The Final Year Told by Those Who Lived It* (New York: The Library of America, 2014).
Rebecca Edwards, "Domesticity versus Manhood Rights: Republicans, Democrats, and 'Family Values' Politics, 1856–1896," in Meg Jacobs, William J. Novak, and Julian E. Zelizer (Eds.), *The Democratic Experiment* (pp. 175–197) (Princeton, NJ: Princeton University Press, 2003).
Daniel Farber, *Lincoln's Constitution* (Chicago, IL: University of Chicago Press, 2003).
Drew Gilpin Faust, *This Republic of Suffering: Death and the American Civil War* (New York: Vintage, 2008).
Eric Foner, *Free Soil, Free Labor, Free Men: The Ideology of the Republican Party before the Civil War* (Oxford, UK: Oxford University Press, 1995).
Eric Foner, *The Fiery Trial: Abraham Lincoln and American Slavery* (New York: W.W. Norton, 2010).

Eric Foner, *Reconstruction: America's Unfinished Revolution: 1863–1877* (New York: HarperPerennial, 2014).

George Fredrickson, *Racism: A Short History* (Princeton, NJ: Princeton University Press, 2016).

Paul Frymer, *Building an American Empire: The Era of Territorial and Political Expansion* (Princeton, NJ: Princeton University Press, 2017).

William Gienapp, *This Fiery Trial: The Speeches of Abraham Lincoln* (Oxford, UK: Oxford University Press, 2002).

Adam Gopnik, "Abraham Lincoln, and the Birth of Stand Your Ground," *The New Yorker*, July 18, 2013.

Michael Hanchard, *The Spectre of Race: How Discrimination Haunts Western Democracy* (Princeton, NJ: Princeton University Press, 2018).

Louis Hartz, *The Liberal Tradition in America* (New York: Harcourt Brace, 1991).

Timothy S. Huebner, *Liberty and Union: The Civil War and Constitutionalism American* (Lawrence, KS: University Press of Kansas, 2016).

Jill Lepore, *These Truths: A History of the United States* (New York: W.W. Norton, 2018).

Theodore J. Lowi, "Bend Sinister: How the Constitution Saved the Republic and Lost Itself: The 2008 James Madison Lecture," *PS: Political Science and Politics*, 42(1), 3–9, 2009.

James McPherson, *Abraham Lincoln and the Second American Revolution* (Oxford, UK: Oxford University Press, 1991).

James McPherson, *Abraham Lincoln* (Oxford, UK: Oxford University Press, 2009).

Herman Melville, *Battle-Pieces and Aspects of the War* (New York: Harper & Brothers, 1866).

Herman Melville, *Billy Budd, Bartleby, and Other Stories* (New York: Penguin Random House, 1986).

William Russell, "The American Correspondence of the *London Times*: Another Letter from Mr. William Russell," *New York Times*, September 4, 1861.

Arthur M. Schlesinger, Jr., *The Cycles of American History* (New York: Mariner Books, 1999).

Ronald C. White, Jr., *Lincoln's Greatest Speech: The Second Inaugural* (New York: Simon & Schuster, 2005).

Garry Wills, *Lincoln at Gettysburg: The Speech that Changed America* (New York: Simon & Schuster, 1992).

Garry Wills, *A Necessary Evil: A History of American Distrust of Government* (New York: Simon & Schuster, 2002).

Brenda Wineapple, *Hawthorne: A Life* (New York: Random House, 2003).

CHAPTER FIVE
POLITICAL THOUGHT AND THE NEW AMERICAN STATE: 1877–1932

Introduction

One of Alexis de Tocqueville's most important observations during his visit to the United States was what he described as the absence of an administrative state: "Certain undertakings interest the entire state and nevertheless cannot be executed because there is no national administration to direct them" (Mansfield, Winthrop, and de Tocqueville, 67, 2000). As a European, Tocqueville anticipated a stronger central state presence. What he found was a nation of "parties and courts" with little else familiar to Europe's more powerful governments. While some have seen a tendency in historians and political scientists to exaggerate the veracity of this observation of Tocqueville's, it has resonated over time because it captures a basic truth about the United States.[1] The "state" – centralized bureaucratic government – came late to America. This was so for historical and philosophical reasons, including a uniquely American aversion to strong government (Kingdon, 1999).

By the middle of the nineteenth century, some of the contours of a modern administrative state were taking form. As the political scientist Richard Bensel noted, the Civil War greatly accelerated this process, modernizing "policies associated with the industrial and financial sectors of the North" (Bensel, 2, 1990). The political capital of Washington, DC transformed from the sleepy, fetid back-water it had long been associated with to something approaching a modern political capital with administrative ambitions. Likewise, Wall Street, the economic capital long imagined by Alexander Hamilton, took on the features of a national center of capital and finance. The particular idiosyncrasies of life in such a capital were captured by Herman Melville in his short story, "Bartleby the Scrivener: A Tale of Wall Street," written in 1853:

> I should have stated before that ground-glass folding doors divided my premises into two parts, one of which was occupied by my scriveners [copiers], the other by myself. ... I resolved to assign Bartleby a corner by the folding doors, but on my side of them, so as to have this quiet man within easy call, in case any trifling thing was to be done. ... I procured a high green folding screen, which might entirely isolate Bartleby from my sight, though not remove him from my voice. And thus, in a manner, privacy and society were conjoined.
>
> (Melville, 111, 1986)

This passage may well be the first in American literature to describe the emergence of the office cubicle. Melville gives this peculiar office structure political meaning; it renders Bartleby, and other similarly situated lower-rung office hands on Wall Street, subjects to the command of a new kind of American leader – the financial executive. The dark, viewless features of Bartlebly's office life shape his activity and help dramatize the kind of "mild despotism" Alexis de Tocqueville wrote about in *Democracy in America*. As a "tale of Wall Street," the surreal quality of the story becomes less opaque as we learn that Bartleby's resistance to this new life, however unsuccessful, emerges out of a simple premise. By refusing to perform the acts associated with this new form of grinding capitalism, Bartleby has made himself not only unwelcome, but also a menace to his environment. "I prefer not to" becomes his mantra throughout the story, and a kind of civil disobedience to the new administrative bureaucracy of the time. Ultimately, Bartleby's refusal to leave the premises of the office makes him the literary equivalent of a proto-"Occupy Wall Street" figure, a person whose societal displacement can only be fought by remaining in place. Lest the reader fail to see the larger connections to the rise of an emergent and equally oppressive bureaucratic state, Melville informs the reader of Bartleby's life prior to his position as scrivener:

> I hardly know whether I should divulge one little item of rumor which came to my ear a few months before the scrivener's disease. Upon what basis it rested, I could never ascertain, and hence how true it is I cannot now tell. But, inasmuch as this vague report has not been without a certain suggestive interest to me, however sad, it may prove the same with some others, and so I will briefly mention it. The report was this: that Bartleby had been a subordinate clerk in the Dead Letter Office at Washington, from which he had been suddenly removed by a change in the administration.
>
> (Melville, 53–54)

Bartleby, like the nation, had gone from one form of repressive bureaucratic regime (the state) to another (the corporation).

That Melville expressed these sentiments in a sense prophesied the kind of state historians would associate with America closer to 50 years later. His prescience underscores not only his skills as a writer, but also as a keen observer of the shift in national politics underway. While American conservatives have been more associated with opposition to the anti-democratic and repressive qualities of big government, liberals have been more apt to criticize the undue powers associated with big business. Melville's political thought saw both entities as deeply troubling to democratic life and human dignity.

The Transcendentalist movement was a counter to the change in scale in American life, with industrialization, urbanization, and capitalism changing the physical and psychological landscape of the country. Bartleby's "I prefer not to" was a version of civil disobedience worthy of Henry David Thoreau, who published his essay "On Civil Disobedience" in 1849, four years before Melville's short story. The nation was changing at mid-century, and would only continue to do so in sharper relief after the Civil War and Reconstruction. As racial retrenchment in the South undid much of the progress effectuated by the Civil War amendments, the new dynamics of rapid immigration, industrialization, a newly focused women's movement, and imperial motivations all made for a new kind of state in America. The politics of reform and reaction would shape the nature of political thought and conflict in the nation over the next fifty years.

Reconstruction's End and the Lessons of *Plessy*

The United States made three critical compromises affecting the future of race relations over the second half of the nineteenth century. The first, coming at the mid-century mark in 1850, was the compromise over the spoils of Mexico and the permissibility of slavery in the newly admitted states. The second was made just after the three-quarter-century mark in 1877, ending Reconstruction and laying the groundwork for racial segregation in the South. Finally, just short of the close of the 1800s, the Supreme Court established the legal right to racial segregation in *Plessy v. Ferguson* (1896), making "separate but equal" the law of the land. The underlying political thought for each was the maintenance of white supremacy – in citizenship rights and in social circles. The *Plessy* decision's one silver lining has long been touted as being Justice John Marshal Harlan's stirring dissent, famous for criticizing the majority opinion's willful rejection of the idea that "There is no caste here."

The Court's decision to deny the plaintiff in the case, Homer Plessy, an African American, from riding in a railcar reserved for whites was premised upon the faulty "compromise" that separate accommodations based upon race were not unconstitutional, provided they were equal. The Court never quite expressed a standard for what this equality would look like, other than that separate accommodations were to be provided for. But Harlan's dissent, one that remains a cornerstone of liberalism's rejection of a racially conscious state, was in fact quite racially conscious. To understand how so, we need to revisit the period's political thought with respect to race.

The early progressivism of the late nineteenth century included arguments for the idea of historical progress among "less advanced" races. The racial essentialism of the period was strengthened by Social Darwinism, and though a cudgel in the hands of white supremacists, it was nonetheless a fundamental belief even among progressive black thinkers and activists such as W.E.B. Du Bois (Appiah, 2014). As the philosopher Kwame Anthony Appiah has written:

> like practically everybody else in his era, [Du Bois] had absorbed the notion, spread by a wide range of European and American intellectuals over the course of the nineteenth century, that race – the division of the world into distinct groups, identifiable by the new biological sciences – was central to social, cultural, and political life.[2]

Harlan was writing in this milieu, and his dissent affirmed its premises. That he did so, like Du Bois, in an effort to reverse the ill effects of racism is without question. That the very racism he sought to address was in many respects fueled by the kind of essentialist logic underpinning his argument in *Plessy* bears examination.

Harlan and Du Bois understood race in terms of "progress" and historical maturation. Northern European racial stock – Anglo-Saxons and Scandinavians – were the best of the lot of the European race – but others (including Southern Europeans, such as Italians) could advance in time. Social scientists also understood race as a useful scientific term for grouping members of the human family into discrete categories – categories based upon certain shared characteristics, ones that included not only physiognomic traits, but cultural ones as well.

"Every true man has pride of race," Harlan declared in his *Plessy* dissent.[3] As a former slave owner, Harlan was now operating on the Court in the interest of removing what he saw as the last vestiges of slavery. But race, in and of itself, was not an odious form of social or biological classification. In fact, the "pride of race" Harlan alluded to was a nod to the idea that members of a particular race had certain enviable characteristics. Where Harlan differed from much of the progressive racism (an ironic juxtaposition to be sure) of his time was in its lack of applicability to the Constitution. "The white race deems itself to be the dominant race in this country," Harlan argued:

> And so it is in prestige, in achievements, in education, in wealth and in power. So, I doubt not, it will continue to be for all time if it remains true to its great heritage and holds fast to the principles of constitutional liberty. But in view of the Constitution, in the eye of the law, there is in this country no superior, dominant, ruling class of citizens. There is no caste here.[4]

Here, Harlan expressly identifies the liberal creed with respect to race – certainly to that point in American history. White supremacy and liberty were hardly incompatible; moreover, appeals to racial justice were buttressed by the acknowledgement of the perpetuation of racial hierarchy. Presumably, Harlan (and other progressives) imagined an American state where liberty was administered without respect to race, believing that the economic and political power of whites would remain undisturbed, given innate white superiority.

Harlan went on to make his case for the unconstitutionality of racial segregation by alluding to (and without condemning) the civic ostracism of persons of Chinese descent living in America:

> There is a race so different from our own that we do not permit those belonging to it to become citizens of the United States. Persons belonging to it are, with few exceptions, absolutely excluded from our country. I allude to the Chinese race. But, by the statute in question, a Chinaman can ride in the same passenger coach with white citizens of the United States, while citizens of the black race in Louisiana, many of whom, perhaps, risked their lives for the preservation of the Union, who are entitled, by law, to participate in the political control of the State and nation, who are not excluded, by law or by reason of their race, from public stations of any kind, and who have all the legal rights that belong to white citizens, are yet declared to be criminals, liable to imprisonment, if they ride in a public coach occupied by citizens of the white race.[5]

By referencing the Chinese Exclusion Act of 1882, Harlan valorizes black citizenship rights over those of Asians – an example of the type of racial triangulation frequently employed historically by elites within the US government to oppose racial progress. The irony here is that the example was employed by Harlan to "benefit" blacks at the expense of members of the Asian American community.[6] Thus, Harlan's historic dissent, one that helped lay the legal basis for the erosion of segregation in America decades later in *Brown v. Board of Education* (1954), was built upon three troubling premises: pride of race; the perpetuation of white superiority; and the exclusion of Chinese Americans from citizenship. With the United States becoming an industrial power in the latter part of the nineteenth century, immigration became a critical part of national discussions relating to the future of the country and the nature of citizenship.

Immigration and the American State

In his influential study of the creation of the modern American state, the political scientist Stephen Skowronek noted: "The years between the nationwide railroad strike of 1877 and the Spanish–American War define an era of labor violence unparalleled in any other industrial nation" (Skowronek, 87, 1982). Skowronek's focus here was on the United States' effort to strengthen its military capacity in an era of internal conflict and external expansion. Labor's radicalization was in part fueled by the harsh new productive imperatives of industrial capitalism, and a labor force increasingly made up of immigrants who were pushing for greater rights for workers. Support for tariffs and restrictions on immigration ran counter to both free market capitalism and the need for low-wage workers. The racialization of the American work force was part of a national political project to shape the nature of labor relations along lines that afforded greater protections for white workers – while enabling the expansion of American industry.

"Those who come as immigrants are the lowest orders of the Chinese population, largely criminal," said Senator James Harvey Slater in 1882. "I believe unless Congress adopts stringent restrictive legislation that multitudes of Chinese laborers – cooly laborers – will immigrate to our Pacific states" (Kramnick and Lowi, 897, 2009). The passage of the Chinese Exclusion Act in 1882 was the end result of this way of thinking – an amalgam of "scientific" racism, nativism, and industrial capitalism's efforts to grow with minimal antagonism. Speeches like Slater's directed the weight of "civilization" against the professed barbarism of Chinese, Irish, and Southeast European immigrants in the latter part of the nineteenth century. The United States Supreme Court explicitly invoked this doctrine in *People v. Hall* in 1854, arguing that the Chinese are a "race of people whom nature has marked as inferior, and who are incapable of progress or intellectual development beyond a certain point, as their history has shown" (Lepore, 325, 2018).

Earlier elite political views of German and Irish immigration were shaped in part by their economic status. Germans, for example, were economically better off and endured less prejudice (Lepore, 209). Religious distinctions among immigrants mattered as well, as much of American political thought reviled Catholicism. Louis Menand, for one, argued that the pragmatist philosopher William James "regarded democracy as the political equivalent of Protestantism" (Menand, 87, 2001). The complexity of views shaping opposition to certain immigrant groups nevertheless followed certain enduring political preferences: the "quality" of their whiteness, Protestantism, and economic status.

What was unique in the case of Chinese immigration, as Daniel J. Tichenor has shown, was that "Unlike their European counterparts, Chinese newcomers were essentially powerless to resist new exclusionary laws, given their lack of political access or leverage in U.S. courts or partisan elections of the nineteenth century" (Tichenor, 11–12, 2002).

Inegalitarian traditions rooted in racial preference formed a contending theory to the liberal idea of an America rooted in democratic values and fairness (Tichenor, 27). In a sense, the hierarchy of liberal ideas was at cross-purposes – the desire to maximize profits in industry while minimizing racial difference and the "dilution" of a white (itself defined along hierarchical lines, beginning with Northern, Protestant Europeans) citizen class points to the complexity of national state development where race is confirmed. Senator Henry Cabot Lodge, debating in favor of a more restrictive immigration law in 1896, argued the following:

> It is found, in the first place, that the illiteracy test will bear most heavily upon the Italians, Russians, Poles, Hungarians, Greeks, and Asiatics, and very lightly, or not at all, upon English-speaking emigrants or Germans, Scandinavians, and French. In other words, the races most affected by the illiteracy test are those whose emigration to this country has begun within the last twenty years and swelled rapidly to enormous proportions, races with which the English-speaking people have never hitherto assimilated, and who are most alien to the great body of the people of the United States.
>
> (Kramnick and Lowi, 911)

The growing movement in phrenology studies and eugenics provided compelling "evidence" that American citizenship was to be increasingly premised upon biologically desirable groups. The political thought of Roger B. Taney was now aided by pseudo-scientific rationales, ones that likewise included racial critiques of Southern and Eastern European immigrants. By 1925, the year of publication for F. Scott Fitzgerald's novel *The Great Gatsby*, the author could evoke in everyday dialogue highbrow notions of "breeding" that marginalized Italians to the "valley of the ashes," and rendered Jews as "kikes" (Fitzgerald, 24, 2004). Political rights conferred to newcomers were dependent on their impact upon the ethno-cultural makeup of the population. This did not exclude groups otherwise perceived as whites. "Whiteness" as a political concept cut both ways, as the historian Matthew Frye Jacobson has pointed out:

> [I]n this period of volatile racial meanings, peoples such as Celts, Italians, Hebrews, and Slavs were becoming less and less white in debates over who should be allowed to disembark on American shores, and yet were becoming whiter and whiter in debates over who should be granted the full rights of citizenship. The discourse of immigration restriction favored a scheme of hierarchically ordered white races, that is, and found some of these sorely wanting in the characteristics required for self-government, whereas naturalization discourse discovered fundamental and unforgiving differences between the white races on the one hand and the hordes of nonwhite Syrian, Turkish, Hindu, and Japanese claimants who were petitioning the courts for citizenship on the other.
>
> (Jacobson, 75, 1999)

It is important to remember that many of these debates were driven as much by questions of labor as they were by notions of racial superiority. Frederick Douglass himself argued, "every hour sees the black man elbowed out of employment by some newly arrived immigrant" (Tichenor, 37). While this position was not an endorsement of racial hierarchy, it did underscore the vitality of labor-based anti-immigration arguments. The rapid pace of industrialization and urbanization after the Civil War transformed the life experience of millions of Americans. A formerly agrarian society was now becoming one shaped by capital and forms of labor more removed from family life, local communities, and traditions. With the arrival of large numbers of immigrants, members of New York's elite, for example, sought to restrict suffrage rights. One such effort was to return to property-based suffrage rights, a form of disenfranchisement designed to strip "lesser" groups from wielding power in the city. New York's elite expressed sympathy with white southerners on the franchise question, with the *Commercial and Financial Chronicle* arguing, "southerners have an ignorant class to deal with, as we have here" (Beckert, 162, 2003). Ironically, urban machine politics tended to be less exclusionary than that found in more elite-based progressivism.

In short, democratic philosophy's pliability was marked by racial, ethnic, and religious classifications with a heightened intensity during the industrial age in America. Suffrage rights were but one aspect of this new reality, one affected by demographic changes related to immigration. Likewise, the persistence of limitations and exclusions on women's suffrage was a source of social, intellectual, and political mobilization in the latter part of the nineteenth century, renewing older debates about gender and democratic citizenship. The distinctiveness of the women's suffrage movement spoke to features of American political thought still beholden to the idea of limited freedom for women in American society.

Late State Development and Women's Rights

The long march to women's suffrage culminated in the passage of the 19th Amendment in 1920. Signed by Woodrow Wilson, one of the greatest transformations in democratic politics was the product of sustained struggle, pragmatic politics, and the emergence of interest group politics. As the historian Brian Balogh has asserted, "the most fundamental shift in the political system between 1900 and 1970 was the emergence of the interest groups as indicators of voter preference" (Balogh, 240, 2003). For example, William James, Sr.'s belief that woman is "man's inferior in passion, his inferior in intellect, and his inferior in physical strength" had been countered, if not displaced, by a critical feature of democratic rights (Menand, 86). An additional shift in national politics was the development of the United States away from a legislative to a presidential republic; this made the presidency the locus for national politics and shaped progressive change in the twentieth century.

Like other forms of progressive historical change in America, the passage of the 19th Amendment represented a partial victory for democracy. The black feminist author bell hooks spoke to this persistent problem:

> The fervor over women's rights generated in the 19th century continued in the 20th century and culminated in the ratification of the 19th Amendment in August 1920 which granted all women the right to vote. In their struggle to win the vote, black women had learned a bitter lesson. They found as they worked for suffrage they saw that many whites saw granting women the right to vote as another way to maintain the oppressive system of white racial imperialism. Southern

white suffragists rallied around a platform that argued that woman suffrage in the South would strengthen white supremacy.

(hooks, 170, 2015)

As was the case with the increase in white male suffrage in the early nineteenth century and the Civil War amendments, passage of the 19th Amendment was an affirmation and betrayal of democratic equality; extension of the franchise was partial and accompanied by contrarian theories of white racial superiority. The universal language of the Amendment created democratic possibilities while masking political realities for black women.

As Jill Lepore put it, pithily, "the Progressive Party was not, in fact, strictly a white man's party; it was also a white woman's party" (Lepore, 387). Teddy Roosevelt's 1912 campaign to regain the presidency made women's suffrage a part of its party platform while acquiescing to black political subordination. African American delegates were denied seats at the Progressive Party convention, for example (Lepore, 387). The new administrative state emergent at the end of the nineteenth century found its locus of power in the American presidency. The progressives' call for more direct democracy while insisting upon expert administration did not extend to black political participation. White women found some traction politically within the progressive movement, although this was restricted to secondary efforts to make the party of Roosevelt more appealing. The black political movement itself developed along similar lines, with black women remaining largely symbolic figures of apolitical domesticity and in subordinate political roles. W.E.B. Du Bois was an important exception, arguing that "the uplift in women is, next to the problem of the color line and the peace movement, our greatest modern cause. When now, two of these movements – women and color combine in one, the combination has deep meaning" (Lewis, 309, 1995).

As Suzanne Marilley put it, "egalitarianism lost out to the popularity of racialist theories and liberals' inclination to think that only educated voters could achieve political equality" (Marilley, 187, 1997). Women's suffrage was undoubtedly an enormous stride towards the fulfillment of democratic ideals. That it was a partial victory in this regard speaks to the long, staggered march towards basic civic equality in America. The right of women to vote was itself subordinated to the cause of abolition for much of the movement's early history. As Daniel Tichenor has written,

"The woman's suffrage movement languished at the periphery of American politics for far longer than the abolitionist campaign" (Skowronek and Glassman, 257, 2007). The incremental, gradualist model of racial and gender equality has been upheld in both conservative, and ostensibly progressive periods in American politics, suggesting a more enduring set of values – held among both elites and the broader population. Indeed, the historian John Pettegrew's research sees the modern origins of terroristic male violence in the United States beginning during the Progressive Era (Pettegrew, 1, 2007).

Perhaps the most relevant historical feature of women's political exclusion has been male social dominance. For Pettegrew and other historians, Darwinian notions of male power shaped this framework; this included a literary and historical tradition of rugged individualism, and a leisure class model that favored violent sport – namely American football. That women's suffrage emerged at the end of this historical track owed more to protest and organization on the part of women than it did to progressivism's inherent support for a variety of forms of human equality. Another important part of the success of the women's suffrage movement was its association with the American war effort during the First World War. The historian Suzanne Lebsock writes:

> With such impressive and determined organization – and an increasing number of states entering the suffrage column – nationwide victory began to look inevitable, and the cause won more friends in high places; President Woodrow Wilson endorsed the amendment in 1918 as a war measure. The mobilization of millions of American women on behalf of the war effort probably helped as well. Food preservation campaigns in particular underscored what suffragists had been arguing all along: There was political significance to what women did at home.
>
> (Lebsock, 53, 1990)

As Indian Removal and westward expansion had been a cornerstone of universal white male suffrage, and the Civil War had been the indispensible event that brought about the end of chattel slavery, so too did violent conflict promote the administrative capacity of the American state to expand democratic rights. As we shall see, beginning with American forays into the Pacific in the middle of the nineteenth century, the United States built an imperial project that took the country from a fledgling and divided republic to the world's most powerful nation within the span of a lifetime. Democratic theory was made up of robust notions of broad civic participation and the expansion of rights, while simultaneously extolling the virtues of the exclusion of foreigners, women, blacks, and indigenous peoples from the political process. As various elements of this constituency of the excluded were brought more into the world of politics – chiefly through organized struggle – a critical rationale for doing so was in demonstrating loyalty and support for the imperial project.

But there was an imagined, hoped for quality to the progressive vision for women's liberation. Yet it lacked a deeper appeal – one captured as well as by any in Toni Morrison's novel *Beloved*. It is the scene where the enslaved Sethe flees her master's plantation with the white woman, Amy Denver – for whom she names her daughter. It is a memorial to the character as much as it is to the world of possibilities – an unrealized dream held within American political thought:

> On a riverbank in the cool of a summer evening two women struggled under a shower of silvery blue. They never expected to see each other again in this world and at the moment couldn't care less. But there on a summer night surrounded by bluefern they did something together appropriately and well. A pateroller would have sniggered to see two throw-away people, two lawless outlaws – a slave and a barefoot whitewoman with unpinned hair – wrapping a ten-minute-old baby in the rags they wore. But no pateroller came and no preacher. The water sucked and swallowed itself beneath them. There was nothing to disturb them at their work. So they did it appropriately and well.
>
> (Morrison, 99–100, 2004)

Throw-away people indeed.

Empire and Democracy: 1850–1920

The *New York Times*' coverage of the arrival of Commodore Matthew Perry's fleet in Japan reveals much about the origin and subsequent development of US empire-building efforts in the nineteenth century. On October 19, 1853, the *Times* reported:

> The object of this visit [Perry] was to be received by the Regent of these famous Islands at his Royal Palace. The honor of this visit may have redounded to his tawny Excellence, but it is certain, such as it was, that the pleasure was all on our side. They are suspicious and very ill at ease. Commodore Perry was carried in a sedan chair. The rest of us gave a specimen of how Yankees, heavily accoutered, can march under a scorched sun on foot. If the Japanese give us a friendly reception, all will be smooth. If not, we will have a far more effective squadron here one of these days, and teach them conformity to Christian manners.[7]

The "Christian manners" to be taught to the "tawny" Japanese was trade: namely, the opening of Japan's markets to American goods. Within roughly six months, Perry, who had arrived in July of 1853, was successful, compelling Japan under threat of force to open its markets and supply coal to American steam ships. The racialized and religious subtext to the *Times'* reporting suggests the relationship between race, Christianity, and capitalism and American political thought in validating the rise of the United States as a world power.

With the acquisition of vast tracts of Mexican territory and its first foray into East Asia with Perry's missions, the United States had by mid-century begun to fulfill Patrick Henry's warning that "Some way or other we must be a great and mighty empire." Henry's fear, articulated at Virginia's ratifying convention in 1788, was about the loss of republican principles. The challenge of balancing empire with self-government would only exacerbate over time. The Civil War would interrupt this march towards American expansion overseas, but by the late nineteenth century, the United States would find itself drawn into a number of foreign interventions.

As John Pettegrew argued, "In every American war effort, we find a close equation between men wanting to experience the extreme danger and violence of battle and the capacity of the state to make war" (Pettegrew, 218). This masculinist impulse, fueled in part by the popularization of mass newspapers and stories of idealized manhood (such as Teddy Roosevelt and the Rough Riders), made war mobilization that much easier. The Spanish–American War in 1898 brought the United States great influence and new forms of dominion over Cuba, Puerto Rico, and the Philippines. Fighting against darker, more "primitive" foes, American forces were also unified in a post-Civil War atmosphere of white racial comity and fraternity. Comparing the 1898 American volunteers' war to the proto-fascist German Freikorps, Pettegrew cites Klaus Theweleit's study to make the case that the "Desire for perpetual war began with hatred of women – primarily their bodies and sexuality – a misogyny stemming from pre-Oedipal fear of dissolution" (Pettegrew, 219). Theodore Roosevelt's family friend Bob Ferguson wrote to Roosevelt's second wife: "No hunting trip so far has ever equaled it in Theodore's eyes" (Pettegrew, 221).

Republican philosophical opposition to war began to erode during this period, before the fateful eclipse of its anti-war premise dissolved nearly entirely with the Second World War. Putting the horrors of the Civil War behind them ("We are all Yankees now") was part of the social and political dynamic that revivified white racial unity – and northern silence against Jim Crow and its own attendant horrors (Pettegrew, 232). Making the connection between the plight of African Americans and US imperialism, W.E.B. Du Bois lamented the loss of policy focus brought about by war:

> The Negro farmer started behind, – started in debt. This was not his choosing, but the crime of this happy-go-lucky nation which goes blundering along with its Reconstruction tragedies, its Spanish war interludes and Philippine matinees, just as though God really were dead.
>
> (Du Bois, 71, 2017)

It was one of President Theodore Roosevelt's great regrets that history's timing left Woodrow Wilson the glory of serving as president during the Great War. The somber odes to war left by Lincoln, for example, had been replaced by greater ballyhoo and institutional support for war. The racial, gendered, and economic imperatives for expanding American markets were part of the philosophical landscape of this period. The intensification of these themes was on the horizon.

"This country does not intend to become involved in this war," Woodrow Wilson told his chief political adviser Edward M. House in early 1917. "We are the only one of the great White nations that is free from war today, and it would be a crime against civilization for us to go in" (Cooper, Jr., 369, 2009). Wilson biographer John Milton Cooper, Jr. doesn't address the racial dimension of Wilson's remarks, but their significance remains. Wilson's progressive philosophy was not unlike Theodore Roosevelt's or others' with respect to America's place in the world – namely, that of the newly preeminent white nation, one destined to lead world affairs. Wilson's hope before the unleashing of unrestricted submarine warfare by Germany was that the United States could somehow manage this leadership role as a bystander to the Great War. When that changed, Wilson pressed for war out of necessity.

With the nation at war, Wilson set aside his domestic policy agenda to concentrate on a full-scale mobilization of the economy and industry. During the war, industrial production increased by 20 percent, daylight saving time was instituted to save fuel, the government took over the railroad system, and massive airplane and ship-building programs were launched. Americans began paying a new income tax and buying Liberty Bonds to pay for the war. Although most of the power the federal government acquired over the economy during the war was based on voluntary cooperation by businesses and individuals, conformity and aggressive patriotism became the order of the day. Private patriotic organizations persecuted dissenters and anyone suspected of political radicalism. Likewise, the administration sponsored Espionage and Sedition Acts that outlawed criticism of the government, the armed forces, and the war effort. Violators of the law were imprisoned or fined, and even mainstream publications were censored or banned. These policies prefigured the emergence of America's national security state that arose after the Second World War. Few presidents changed the nature of democratic governance at home as did Wilson during the crisis of the First World War. It would lay down a template for the erosion of democratic freedoms in subsequent conflicts, including the Second World War, the Cold War, and the War on Terror.

In *The New Freedom* (1913), Wilson had argued that "Freedom today is something more than being let alone. The program of a government of freedom must in these days be positive, not merely negative" (Kramnick and Lowi, 1113). But Wilson had written that before the United States became the world's greatest power. That new position made "being let alone" a powerful and increasingly difficult democratic ideal during times of war. Within a generation, Americans would never know a time outside of perpetual war – a time of imminent danger, potential nuclear threat, or terror. And it would be the government of positive action that would remind them of these dangers.

The Progressive State Arrives

The historian Jill Lepore succinctly summed up the difference between progressivism and its progenitor, populism. "Populists believed that the system was broken; Progressives believed that the government could fix it" (Lepore, 364). This distinction suggested a shift in democratic ideals. Progressives wanted a government of experts who would direct policies towards the public good. Populists, on the other hand, had an innate distrust of expertise and administrative power. Notwithstanding their diversity of theories and political leaders, progressives did have a unifying and radical bent; they had an unfailing desire to reorder constitutional principles along executive rather than legislative lines. Perhaps the period's most important theorist, Herbert Croly, argued that "the legislature represents those minor phases of public opinion and conscience to demand some vehicle of expression" (Croly, 301, 1915). The executive branch – namely, the president – was to command the responsibilities of the nation's major initiatives.

These initiatives were directed towards reform and countering the rise of unfettered capitalism; executives were thought less prone to corruptibility than legislatures, and so a new relationship between presidents and the public began. "The absence of effective state, and especially, national, restraint upon unfair money getting has tended to create a small class of enormously wealthy and economically powerful men," argued then former President Theodore Roosevelt in 1910 (Kramnick and Lowi, 1091). Roosevelt, like Croly, wanted Hamiltonian national power to drive Jeffersonian outcomes – a more democratic and fair system where the masses of people were protected from the undue influence of both public and private power. As James T. Kloppenberg has written, "The association between Croly and [Roosevelt] was close, and the lines of influence ran in both directions, from their first contact in 1910 until after the election of 1912" (Kloppenberg, 314, 1986).

The executive-centered strand of progressivism was in part a response to the shift in government power and resources to the presidency as much as it was an advocacy for that change in institutional relations. Reform leaders who sought broad societal changes in civic and economic life, such as Jane Addams, understood that shifting national priorities was likely to come at the hand of an American president, rather than Congress. Black progressives such as W.E.B. Du Bois were pulled in a number of directions because of this new set of arrangements. In 1912, Du Bois had written to President Woodrow Wilson: "We received from you a promise of justice and sincere endeavor to forward [black] interests. We need scarcely to say that you have grievously disappointed us" (Cooper, Jr., 361). By 1917, he was writing in *The Crisis*, "If this is OUR country, then this is OUR war," offering his support for the First World War (Cooper, Jr., 408).

Support for America's entry into the Great War was an equally compelling, if not troubling, proposition for the nation's women. Pacifists like Addams had to square their opposition to the war with the need to "prove" one's loyalty and support for America's larger role in the world. Thus, the case for democratic expansion at home was tied to American expansion and increased power abroad – a dialectic of sorts that shaped the nation's foreign policy well into the twentieth century. It was a particularly precarious position for women whose improved standing in the Progressive Era "rested on the idea that women were dependent, not only on men, but on the state" (Lepore, 382).

"The idea of democracy is a wider and fuller idea than can be exemplified in the state even at its best," John Dewey wrote in 1927. "To be realized it must affect all modes of human association, the family, the school, industry, religion" (Kramnick and Lowi, 1036). Dewey's recognition of "social democracy" as equal to political democracy was a critical contribution of the period. Much of the progressive effort to transform economic relationships in the United States involved a reorientation in thinking about rights, community, and the nature of political leadership. The challenge was moving American political thought away from, even temporarily, its hold on individualist notions of freedom and rights. Managing this was easier said than done, as women, African Americans, Native Americans, labor, and immigrants, by way of example, were engaged in struggles with the state that sought recognition on the basis of their group status. What would later emerge as "identity politics" – an expression often used to disparage expansive notions of community and democratic rights – had strong ties to the teachings of progressives like Dewey, who wanted to reverse the relationship between the government and its citizens. "Fraternity, liberty, and equality isolated from communal life are hopeless abstractions," he wrote in *The Public and Its Problems* (Kramnick and Lowi, 1039).

That much of this instruction in challenging conventional notions of American liberty would come from the presidency should come as no surprise. As we shall see, the New Deal was as much a set of new democratic propositions as it was a collection of programs. By the time Franklin Delano Roosevelt became president, the United States had experienced a swing towards more progressive government – and a failed conservative response that culminated in the onset of the Great Depression. FDR and New Deal liberalism had an unprecedented opportunity to shape politics along new lines. Both Theodore Roosevelt and Woodrow Wilson governed in periods of industrial capitalism's widely perceived connection to democracy and public spiritedness. The excesses of this order opened the doors to considerable reform, but those doors would not be as open to new institutional arrangements as they would be in 1932 when FDR came to power – the subject of the next chapter.

Conclusion

In many ways, Herman Melville's "Bartleby the Scrivener" (1853) and F. Scott Fitzgerald's *The Great Gatsby* (1925) are the literary bookends to the America defined by Wall Street and new money. Both works are "tales of Wall Street" – with *Gatsby*'s Nick Carraway playing a different kind of passive role in Fitzgerald's novel – that of admiring observer and chronicler. The small and closely quartered world of Melville's Wall Street had grown considerably over the ensuing decades – and with it, the rise of a new tragic story in American life: the death of unbridled optimism. "Can't repeat the past? Why of course you can!" Gatsby tells Nick (Fitzgerald, 110). It is perhaps his most beautiful and sadly held conviction.

As the political theorist Wilson Carey McWilliams wrote about the 1920s, "the pursuit of wealth reached a new intensity, and the demand behind it was for immediate rather than distant rewards" (McWilliams,

509, 1973). What Fitzgerald was able to perceive was that even old money did not guarantee fulfillment in a country whose ethos was premised upon a perpetual longing – the "pursuit of happiness." The verdict is rendered by Nick, who has discerned something about the nature of Tom and Daisy Buchanan that cuts to the core of acquisitiveness' fundamental emptiness:

> They weren't happy, and neither of them had touched the chicken or the ale – and yet they weren't unhappy either. There was an unmistakable air of natural intimacy about the picture, and anybody would have said they were conspiring together.
>
> (Fitzgerald, 145)

The period before the greatest modern transformation in American politics was one of immense contradictions: a rebuke to modernity amid massive technological change; a denial of social upheaval even as the country was being defined by increasing numbers of Americans born in other countries, living in cities, and less defined by traditional gender roles than in any other time. That these changes were overseen by a new administrative state was unique to American history. In short order, the full weight of that state would be engaged in addressing an economic depression and a second world war. The totality of these struggles would alter American politics for the next half-decade, with liberalism the defining political ideology in domestic and foreign policy. This new liberal state would not abandon older, more traditional attachments – foremost of these being white supremacy and patriarchy.

Those enduring features of American life would more forthrightly be addressed several decades into this new ideological regime – with an attendant reordering of politics necessitating a reversal of sorts, away from liberalism. The struggle to create a progressive state that could engage the imperatives of interest-group politics defined by race or gender was defined by compromise and delay over the ensuing years. The price of delay would lead to an upheaval in the social order with few parallels in the nation's history. But first, the political imperative was to address an economic crisis unparalleled in the nation's history – and not long after, an international crisis threatening global stability and democratic government on a global scale. The gaping hole of racial and gender equality within the liberal system was part of why the new struggle against poverty, fascism, and despotism was fought with such irony and policy limitations. But this had been the story of American political development all along.

Notes

1. See Theda Skocpol, for example: "What Tocqueville Missed," *Slate*, November 15, 1996. https://slate.com/news-and-politics/1996/11/what-tocqueville-missed.html.
2. Kwame Anthony Appiah, "Race in the Modern World," *Foreign Affairs*, 94(2), 1–8, 2015.
3. www.law.cornell.edu/supremecourt/text/163/537#writing-USSC_CR_ 016 3_0537_ZD.
4. Ibid.
5. Ibid.
6. Kim, Claire Jean, "The Racial Triangulation of Asian Americans," *Politics & Society*, 27(1), 105–138, 1999.
7. "The Japan Expedition – Commodore Perry at the Lee-Choo Isles," *New York Times*, October 19, 1853.

References

Kwame Anthony Appiah, *Lines of Descent: W.E.B. Du Bois and the Emergence of Identity* (Cambridge, MA: Harvard University Press, 2014).
Kwame Anthony Appiah, "Race in the Modern World," *Foreign Affairs*, 94(2), 1–8, 2015.
Brian Balogh, "Mirror of Desires: Interest Groups, Elections, and the Targeted Style in Twentieth-Century America," in Meg Jacobs, William J. Novak, and Julian E. Zelizer (Eds.), *The Democratic Experiment* (pp. 222–249) (Princeton, NJ: Princeton University Press, 2003).
Sven Beckert, "Democracy in the Age of Capital: Contesting Suffrage Rights in Gilded Age New York," in Meg Jacobs, William J. Novak, and Julian E. Zelizer (Eds.), *The Democratic Experiment* (pp. 146–174) (Princeton, NJ: Princeton University Press, 2003).
Richard Bensel, *Yankee Leviathan: The Origins of Central State Authority in America, 1859–1877* (Cambridge, UK: Cambridge University Press, 1990).
John Milton Cooper, Jr., *Woodrow Wilson* (New York: Alfred A. Knopf, 2009).
Herbert Croly, *Progressive Democracy* (New York: Macmillan, 1915).
W.E.B. Du Bois, *The Souls of Black Folk* (New York: CreateSpace, 2017).
F. Scott Fitzgerald, *The Great Gatsby* (New York: Scribner, 2004).

bell hooks, *Ain't I a Woman: Black Women and Feminism* (New York: Routledge, 2015).

Matthew Frye Jacobson, *Whiteness of a Different Color: European Immigrants and the Alchemy of Race* (Cambridge, MA: Harvard University Press, 1999).

Claire Jean Kim, "The Racial Triangulation of Asian Americans," *Politics & Society*, 27(1), 105–138, 1999.

John Kingdon, *America the Unusual* (New York: Worth Publishers, 1999).

James T. Kloppenberg, *Uncertain Victory: Social Democracy and Progressivism in European and American Thought, 1870–1920* (Oxford, UK: Oxford University Press, 1986).

Isaac Kramnick and Theodore Lowi, *American Political Thought: A Norton Anthology* (New York: W.W. Norton, 2009).

Suzanne Lebsock, *Women, Politics, and Change* (Louise A. Tilly and Patricia Gurin, Eds.) (Washington, DC: Russell Sage Foundation, 1990).

Jill Lepore, *These Truths: A History of the United States* (New York: W.W. Norton, 2018).

David Levering Lewis, *W.E.B. Du Bois, 1868–1919: Biography of a Race* (New York: Owl Books, 1995).

Harvey Mansfield, Debra Winthrop, and Alexis de Tocqueville, *Democracy in America* (Chicago, IL: University of Chicago Press, 2000).

Suzanne M. Marilley, *Women's Suffrage and the Origins of Liberal Feminism in the United States, 1820–1920* (Cambridge, MA: Harvard University Press, 1997).

Wilson Carey McWilliams, *The Idea of Fraternity in America* (Berkeley, CA: University of California Press, 1973).

Herman Melville, *Billy Budd, Bartleby, and Other Stories* (New York: Penguin Random House, 1986).

Louis Menand, *The Metaphysical Club: A Story of Ideas in America* (New York: Farrar, Straus, and Giroux, 2001).

Toni Morrison, *Beloved* (New York: Vintage Books, 2004).

John Pettegrew, *Brutes in Suits: Male Sensibility in America, 1890–1920* (Baltimore, MD: Johns Hopkins University Press, 2007).

Theda Skocpol, "What Tocqueville Missed," *Slate*, November 15, 1996. Retrieved from https://slate.com/news-and-politics/1996/11/what-tocqueville-missed.html

Stephen Skowronek, *Building a New American State: The Expansion of National Administrative Capacities, 1877–1920* (Cambridge, UK: Cambridge University Press, 1982).

Stephen Skowronek and Matthew Glassman (Eds.), *Formative Acts: American Politics in the Making* (Philadelphia, PA: University of Pennsylvania Press, 2007).

Daniel J. Tichenor, *Dividing Lines: The Politics of Immigration Control in America* (Princeton, NJ: Princeton University Press, 2002).

CHAPTER SIX
REDEFINING RIGHTS: 1932–1980

Introduction

In August of 1932, Adolf A. Berle wrote Franklin Delano Roosevelt a memo arguing that he would have to soon articulate a philosophy of government to guide the remainder of his campaign for the presidency, and to provide direction to his administration. An early member of Roosevelt's "Brain Trust," Berle wrote: "In a word, it is necessary to do for this system what Bismarck did for the German system in 1880, as a result of conditions not unlike these" (Ambar, 141–142, 2012). Despite considerable differences of opinion among FDR's advisers, it was evident the government had to take a proactive stance and address not only the Great Depression, but the laissez-faire policies that had led to the concentration of wealth and failure to address massive unemployment.

FDR's task was to do this within the context of a large, diverse, multi-racial and multiethnic democratic republic, one lacking the kind of authoritarian state tradition Bismarck inherited. The outlines of the New Deal could be seen in Roosevelt's Commonwealth Club Address in San Francisco in September of 1932. In it, he called for a "reappraisal of values," arguing that the early debates between Alexander Hamilton and Thomas Jefferson were not suited to the crisis facing the nation at the time.[1] This was because of the birth of modern industrial capitalism and the resultant concentration of power in the hands of a few large corporations and business interests. Roosevelt did not have to introduce his approach without precedent. In many respects, the New Deal's programs and philosophy were the culmination of nearly 50 years of Populist and Progressive Era reform efforts.

"Where Jefferson had feared the encroachment of political power on the lives of individuals, [Woodrow] Wilson knew that the new power was financial," Roosevelt said.[2] FDR had the advantage of a progressive history; he also faced the daunting prospect of an economic crisis far greater than the ones that had previously confronted policymakers. In addition, addressing the crisis required navigating Democratic Party politics. In short, "economics was used to finesse the most profound internal contradiction of the now hegemonic Democratic party: half northern liberalism and half southern feudalism" (Kramnick and Lowi, 1120, 2009). Southern authoritarianism was rooted in systemic racism and a hands-off approach by first Republican and later Democratic presidential administrations towards white supremacy in the region. The Great Depression was not unlike other first-order crises in American history in this regard: it necessitated a confrontation with the nation's espoused democratic values and its long history of racial oppression. The pattern of compromise continued, with expedient political concerns taking precedent.

As Ira Katznelson wrote in his history of the New Deal, "The United States possessed many of the same features Hannah Arendt was soon to associate with the rise of totalitarianism" (Katznelson, 39, 2013). That racism, imperialism, and domestic terror functioned historically in an otherwise democratic state gave Roosevelt and his Brain Trust a historic template to consider the politics of radical change – a veritable reservoir of certainty in a period marked by its absence. That the New Deal coalition began to collapse when this historical pattern was directly attacked at mid-century reflected a fundamental change in the nation's politics, as I will soon discuss.

In making his case to the nation at the Commonwealth Club, Roosevelt made an astonishing admission. "A glance at the situation today only too clearly indicates," he began, "that equality of opportunity no longer exists."[3] Had FDR been limiting his conclusion to the then present circumstances, it would have been a less striking statement. On the contrary, Roosevelt's painstakingly detailed and historically based speech was purposefully designed to show that the Depression was but part of a longer history of economic inequality's rise. The reappraisal of values he referred to required a reckoning with American political history, one that presumed sufficient resources and their equitable distribution to meet the basic needs of the people. This was no longer the case. Moreover, Roosevelt had to affirm that somehow, reorienting the government towards economic equality and the public good would not fundamentally alter the core values of the United States.

"Faith in America, faith in our tradition of personal responsibility, faith in our institutions, faith in ourselves demands that we recognize the new demands of the old social contract," he said.[4] While Berle may have written the speech, in the end it was Roosevelt's optimism and re-telling of the American story that provided a roadmap for a different kind of state than the one he inherited. The new social contract would involve a Second Bill of Rights, a reworking of Jeffersonian ideals. The struggle over the rights of African Americans and the role of women in this system would be a considerable part of this new chapter in American political thought.

Race, Gender, and the Clash of Values

In his January State of the Union Address in 1944, FDR delivered a speech on a "Second Bill of Rights." With considerable progress made in the Second World War, and an economy in recovery from the Great Depression, Roosevelt sought to expand upon his earliest vision of government delivered in San Francisco 12 years earlier. As he referenced in his Commonwealth Club Address, it was the industrial expansion of America's economy that had precipitated a need for a new evaluation of the government's responsibilities. "Necessitous men are not free men," Roosevelt told the nation, before enumerating the right to a job, food, clothing, freedom of competition, a decent home, medical care, security in old age, and a good education (Kramnick and Lowi, 1191).

These ideals became promises in the mind of liberals over time – perhaps unfulfilled ones, but promises nonetheless. The only group mentioned were farmers, although Roosevelt included a powerful line suggestive of more: "We have accepted, so to speak, a second Bill of Rights under which a new basis of security and prosperity can be established for all – regardless of station, race, or creed" (Kramnick and Lowi, 1191, 2009). The interposition of this line offered hope that African Americans would not be excluded from the benefits of such a Bill of Rights; but blacks had now fought, quite recently, in two great American wars where the protections of the first Bill of Rights did not apply to them at home. And women were nowhere to be mentioned. What new hope could be found in this revised affirmation of rights?

To start, the hope was that in the sheer exercise of political thought anew, the United States might undertake a more fundamental "reappraisal of values," including its history of racial and gender-based discrimination. As the political scientist Brian Stipelman has argued, the New Deal was an instance, perhaps the most compelling instance in American history since its founding, of democratic theory in practice, where our leaders were theorists (or became theorists because they were leaders) (Stipelman, 8, 2012). The darker side of this revelation is that American political thought, with rare exception, has made little space for considerations of white supremacy and patriarchy as acceptable forms within the nation's set of governing arrangements.

As I'll explore, the New Deal was in many respects an impediment to the attainment of rights and economic protections for African Americans. Nevertheless, Kevin J. McMahon's study of Roosevelt's presidency offers an indirect argument for the pragmatic protection of rights along racial lines – namely through the judiciary:

[The] civil rights decisions [of the Roosevelt Court] are the byproducts of an institutional mission – embraced by the Court – that was significantly shaped by what I call the "judicial policy" of the Roosevelt administration, a policy that was itself a consequence of FDR's management of divisions within the Democratic Party and of his construction of the modern presidency.

(McMahon, 4, 2004)

The "activist" turn taken by the Court that led to *Brown v. Board of Education* (1954) and other decisions was not an act of happenstance, but one carefully constructed during the Roosevelt years. This is a reasonable assessment, but it does not account for the policy-based history that restricted the benefits of the New Deal to whites for decades; nor does it account for the abdication of women's rights as part of the New Deal policy framework. Much of the reassessment of FDR and the New Deal has been based on contemporary studies of the policy-making and implementation process established under Roosevelt. These new accounts of the New Deal years and its theory have been led by the work of Ira Katznelson (Katznelson, 2005).

As Katznelson has written:

> [A]t the very moment when a wide array of public policies was providing most white Americans with valuable tools to advance their social welfare – insure their old age, get good jobs, acquire economic security, build assets, and gain middle-class status – most black Americans were left behind or left out.
>
> (Katznelson, 23, 2005)

This was possible because New Deal policies were implemented at the local level, allowing southern states to set up discriminatory applications of the new economic rights afforded to citizens. Invariably, the vast majority of African Americans were excluded. Once again, the philosophy of "states' rights" had been utilized to bifurcate the socio-economic and political advantages of being an American into racially restrictive camps. The enduring aspect of this practice made the ordinary democratic practice of compromise a uniquely oppressive form of policymaking – going all the way back to the nation's founding.

Under Labor Secretary Frances Perkins – a radical choice at the time, by any measure – the New Deal did provide for modest gains for American women in the work force. With roots in the progressive movements of the early twentieth century, more women worked in the New Deal and in a variety of political organizations during this period than any time before; they formed an intellectual and political network that shaped the status of women within government and the Democratic Party for years to come.[5] Nevertheless, while employment and other benefits were afforded to white women, millions of black women were effectively blocked from considerable benefits in the South, where domestic workers were excluded.

But as Katznelson has shown, even many whites were sacrificed in an effort to bar African Americans from the economic benefits of the

New Deal – a compromise that created "a form of policy apartheid" (Katznelson, 43, 2005). While many blacks resisted these efforts through the formation of secret unions in the South, the deck was stacked heavily against them (Kendi, 337, 2016). In a country steeped in the political traditions of racial exclusion and patriarchy, there was little appetite among liberal white office holders to enforce progressive reform without succumbing to racial discrimination and the marginalization of women. Black women – as had been the case historically – were the most vulnerable, a byproduct of American political thought dating to Thomas Jefferson's *Notes on the State of Virginia* that rendered them disposable and subhuman.

The great continuity in American political life had been forms of expanded political and economic rights with varying degrees of exclusion for blacks, women, and indigenous peoples. Underscoring this categorical discrimination was a system of market, and later industrial capitalism that fueled the nation's growth. And when the greatest assault on that system's unchecked powers was made, it too made concessions to the old ethos of compromise on racial grounds rooted in white supremacy. At mid-century, a more powerful resistance to this system would be born before ushering in an era of revolutionary politics, one compelling the nation to make more fundamental changes at the risk of losing not only the legitimacy of the state at home and abroad, but also the very order of things that had made compromise so sought after all along.

Truman, Eisenhower, and the New Resistance

When Harry Truman became President of the United States upon the death of Franklin Roosevelt, the outlines of a Cold War with the Soviet Union were already evident. The Soviet Union had a military hold over the eastern portion of Europe formerly held by Germany, the result of enormous human sacrifices over several years of war on its soil. That conflict – between fascist and communist ideologies – was replaced by that between capitalism (often read as democracy) and communism (often read as totalitarianism). The greatest tension within the United States' opposition to anti-democratic governments around the world resided in the fact that much of its own country functioned under authoritarian rule (Mickey, 2015).

The dominant liberal ideological framework of a rights-based democratic society had always been at odds with white supremacy in America. But now that once-internal political reality had become fodder for contestation against the entire American political system by both the Soviet Union and those colonized nations on the brink of political independence. The Truman administration attempted to resolve this dilemma by making two concessions. The first was to devote enormous economic and administrative resources to establishing a national security state to confront Soviet power in Europe and in the so-called Third World. The second concession was to begin the slow dismantling of the most visible racist structures within the American political system – those that made the United States particularly vulnerable to ideological criticism from states identified within the socialist bloc.

Yet, as Ibram X. Kendi has written, "Gallop pollsters found that only 6 percent of White Americans thought [African American] rights should be secured" in 1947; this was in response to Truman's Committee on Civil Rights, convened to address this underlying problem in American democracy (Kendi, 355). Truman would go on to insist on the desegregation of the United States armed forces (1948) and support anti-lynching legislation and the enactment of a new Civil Rights Act – one that would reverse decades of Jim Crow politics in the American South. As the *New York Times* reported at the time, the proposals were not without considerable opposition:

> Forty-nine South Carolina legislators denounced this program last week as "repugnant." In a similar criticism, Senator James O. Eastland of Mississippi proposed that the Solid South withhold all its electoral votes to make possible the election of a "distinguished Southerner."[6]

Despite the successful desegregation of the military, Truman's proposals were largely beaten back – in part because northern liberal Democrats were unwilling to risk the New Deal's precious political coalition over the cause of civil rights. Even with this moderate approach, the fissures within the Democratic Party were evident, and the beginning of the re-orientation of the party and its power in the South was underway. As Mary L. Dudziak noted in her groundbreaking work, Truman's motives were connected to the hope that black

Democratic voters would outnumber white defections – while providing the necessary pro-democracy message so needed to "win hearts
and minds" of newly independent countries around the world (Dudziak, 26, 2000).

In 1948, Strom Thurmond and the Dixiecrats bolted the Democratic Party and began the movement of southern whites away from
the party. The New Deal coalition faced open opposition among longstanding stalwarts like Lyndon Johnson, whose maiden speech in the
Senate in 1949 ("We of the South") reflected the deepest and most
racialist interpretations of states' rights familiar to American politics
(Caro, 2003). Such fractures did reflect recognition that the advance
of black rights in the South was energized, if not imminent. By the
time Eisenhower would be inaugurated in 1953, the nation's politics
had shifted, with a newly born conservative movement poised to provide ideological cover for southern opposition to civil rights. But the
Truman years had heartened black activists and white progressives that
perhaps the nation might be poised to address its historic system of
racial injustice. That the forces of moderation – including more overt
reactionary elements – would work to preserve the politics of racial
hierarchy at mid-century was suggestive that ordinary politics was
incapable of upending the system, let alone replacing it. The politics of
moderation was evident even in their aesthetic evaluation of the Black
Freedom Struggle. The *New York Times'* first piece on Dr. Martin
Luther King, Jr. is striking in this regard:

> Dr. King is a rather soft-spoken man with a learning and maturity
> far beyond his twenty-seven years. His clothes are in conservative
> good taste and he has a small trim mustache. He heads an upper-
> middle class group of Negro Baptists with dignity and restraint.[7]

This genteel portrayal of King was in keeping with the *Times'* and
most of liberal white America's unease over the possibility of swift
change with respect to race relations. President Eisenhower was
expressly skeptical of Truman's move to desegregate the armed services, and he later expressed both legal skepticism and personal dismay
over the Supreme Court's ruling in *Brown* (Riley, 178–181, 1999).
Brown's premise itself was a moderate interpretation – or more precisely, an evasion of constitutional principles. It was not based on the
14th Amendment, but rather a sociological conception of black rights.

Segregation contributed to a psychological sense of inferiority among African Americans, and as such, was an inherent violation of the idea of "separate but equal" established in *Plessy v. Ferguson* (1896). As Charles Ogletree argued, "In its solicitude toward southern (and many northern whites) in refusing to describe segregation as an evil, the Brown decision ignores the restorative function of our legal system" (Ogletree, 308, 2004).

In addition to basing the decision on less than expressed constitutional rights, the Warren Court allowed for the gradual implementation of desegregation – employing the term "with all deliberate speed" in its decision. The conservative recognition, if not enforcement, of black rights was part of a longer history, dating from the Emancipation Proclamation and Reconstruction period. Black activists used the *Brown* decision to advocate for the enforcement of desegregation in education – and elsewhere – giving direction and life to what was strictly speaking a legal ruling, not a political commitment. This was true in President Eisenhower's decision to defend federal law in the wake of *Brown*. As Sidney Milkis and Daniel Tichenor have written:

> If [Eisenhower] had failed to act in the face of Governor Faubus's defiance of a court order, he would have yielded to every segregationist governor the right to break the law. Eisenhower's penalty for failing to grasp the weight of the simmering civil rights revolution was that when he did act, he was forced to deploy massive military power domestically.
>
> (Milkis and Tichenor, 142, 2019)

That American presidents have traditionally risked potentially greater forms of political uncertainty, including the invitation of major social disruption, demonstrates the powerful history of ideological commitments to white supremacy. Eisenhower's specific political commitments in this instance were related to his role as president and commander-in-chief; that an American state was standing in defiance of his executive authority was the preeminent motivation for defending the enforcement of the *Brown* decision, dispassionate about doing so though he was.

Thus, even amid the transformation in de jure social relations between African Americans and whites, the strategic effort to preserve order and uphold institutional authority took precedence over more direct reevaluations of the nation's past. Indeed, the brutal murder of Emmett Till did not prevent the presentation of the civil rights movement to the president as a byproduct of opaque forces of communism operating within the United States (Branch, 182, 1988). Thus, the political project of ensuring equal citizenship for African Americans involved questions of preserving domestic tranquility as much as they did those of justice. The mid-century "consensus" between the Democratic and Republic parties involved the acceptance (by and large) of most of the policies of the New Deal; in foreign affairs, it was the policy of containment and opposition to the rise of the Soviet Union and its bloc of allies. Black political leaders and activists alike would have to contend with these priorities – shielding their leaders, programs, and strategies from accusations of disloyalty and radicalism.

American Conservative Thought at Mid-Century

Most Americans familiar with the history of the conservative journal *The National Review* know that its most iconic line came from its first issue. *The National Review*, William F. Buckley, Jr. wrote, "stands athwart history, yelling Stop!"[8] It was a punchy line, one making the implicit argument that the changes apace in the nation – most assuredly those connected with the New Deal and the nascent civil rights movement – were the work of government moving too far and too fast. But the sentence before it made a different, and for the purpose of understanding the history of American political thought more striking, argument. "The launching of a conservative weekly journal of opinion in a country widely assumed to be a bastion of conservatism at first glance looks like a work of supererogation," Buckley wrote, "rather like publishing a royalist weekly within the walls of Buckingham Palace."[9]

Buckley was, in short, belittling the notion that America was then, and had long been, a conservative polity. *The National Review*, he continued, "is out of place because, in its maturity, literate America rejected conservatism in favor of radical social experimentation."[10] The new radicalism, was conservatism; at least in a nation that had given up its basic conservative ethos. And what was that? Government should limit its role as much as possible, from the sphere of economics and private affairs. And liberties could and should be protected for individuals, not groups. The underlying – and, in time, stated – premise was that African

Americans and others, were not afforded special protections outside what the government gave them as de facto citizens. That the status of blacks in the United States was not equal in form or the application of rights was essentially a private matter (undoubtedly owing to black inferiority).

Buckley said as much:

> The central question that emerges – and it is not a parliamentary question or a question that is answered by merely consulting a catalog of the rights of American citizens, born Equal – is whether the White community in the South is entitled to take such measures as are necessary to prevail, politically and culturally, in areas in which it does not predominate numerically? The sobering answer is Yes – the White community is so entitled because, for the time being, it is the advanced race. It is not easy, and it is unpleasant, to adduce statistics evidencing the median cultural superiority of White over Negro: but it is fact that obtrudes, one that cannot be hidden by ever-so-busy egalitarians and anthropologists.[11]

Buckley's form of conservatism was not unfamiliar to American political history. The argument that the "rights of American citizens" – including the most basic Jeffersonian principle that all men are "born Equal" – could be set aside suggests that white supremacy was a value of deeper resonance than democracy. The arresting of history that *The National Review*, and in a sense, mid-century American conservatism, called for was rooted in this premise.

An earlier, and equally vital, focus of Buckley's (and later, American conservatism's) was that of religion. In *God and Man at Yale*, Buckley saw forces hostile to Christianity, and religion more generally, at hand. This was based in part upon Buckley's careful assessment of the Department of Religion's course offerings, personal religious leanings of its faculty, and student assessments, vague as they were in the early 1950s. Buckley contended that Yale had eschewed Christianity in favor of a laissez-faire education that may as well have adopted communism, socialism ("the blood brother of Marxism"), and polygamy, all of equal value to the student experience as their more traditional counterparts (Buckley, 210, 1986). What Buckley (and conservatives) saw taking place at Yale was the subversion of American values – read as those long established by white, Christian, male, heterosexual, and monogamous (supporting, if not acting) individuals. In brief, society was changing.

Buckley saw this well before the dramatic cultural shifts were evident in the 1960s, and he was aghast. That this sociocultural conservatism was coupled with an ethno-political form of racism marked out a divide between conservatism and liberalism, where, at least ostensibly, cultural diversity and racial equality remained esteemed, if not deeply historical American values. Indeed, *The National Review* and *God and Man at Yale* had served as templates for affirming conservative values – a bildungsroman of sorts for the conservative movement. In 1960, Barry Goldwater's *The Conscience of a Conservative* would build on these narratives, making such texts almost prerequisites for running for political office from the right. Beyond academia, Goldwater placed blame on the American media class for marginalizing the voice of conservatives. And he sought to restore the nation to a pre-New Deal footing – first as a United States Senator, and then as the Republican Party nominee for the presidency in 1964. "My aim is not to pass laws," he wrote in his 1960 treatise. "My aim is to repeal them" (Kramnick and Lowi, 1263).

Goldwater's ascendancy was a response to the liberalism of the New Deal state, but also the prevarications of the Eisenhower administration, which was seen by many on the right as too accommodationist. As William E. Leuchtenburg has written, "Even after Eisenhower entered the White House, the Republican right still saw him as a closet Roosevelt follower, in part because he was so frequently linked to FDR" (Leuchtenburg, 47, 2009). It was Eisenhower who would later upbraid Goldwater for his "extremism in the defense of liberty" line delivered in his 1964 speech accepting the Republican Party nomination. The push for a more authentic conservatism was well underway.

The 1950s were thus years of transition for American conservatives. It was the decade when Ronald Reagan left the Democratic Party, if not his heroic attachments to FDR (Wills, 86, 2000). The Republican Party was in power in the White House, but much less so in Congress, and New Deal liberalism still had sway with the general public. But new voices were emerging. As the Black Freedom Struggle grew in intensity and the decade produced new fights on issues of race, conservatism became more identified with white sociopolitical stability – and the Republican Party an institutional bulwark against radical change. Keeping racial upheaval beneath the surface was the work of both political parties, however, and it would take more explosive action to radically shift the nation's attention away from the Cold War and foreign affairs to more domestic affairs. It would be less of a choice, and more of a compulsion, that the politics of the nation's leaders began to address, however reluctantly, what the Swedish economist Gunnar Myrdal had labeled "An American Dilemma" (Myrdal, 1944).

Black Political Thought and the Stakes of Political Change

Black political thought in the United States encompassed a number of political philosophies by the 1950s. The first was the classical rights-based liberalism of the country – long characterized by support for religious freedom, social equality, respect for civil liberties, and the protection of property rights. But black liberalism had been, from its inception, more radical, even within the context of conservative forms of liberalism. This was because black intellectuals and the mass of African American people had to account for inequality rooted in racial hierarchy. This meant economic, political, and social rights could not be separated from racial and group politics.

The liberalism of the United States had long been insufficient for providing equality among its citizens; this included the most basic forms of equality presumed to be provided for all citizens – namely, the right to vote and serve on juries. This is why Martin Luther King, Jr. reserved a good deal of his public criticism for those white moderates whose resistance to racial progress was often tied to liberal values of moderation, deliberation, and order. In his Letter from a Birmingham Jail (1963), King writes:

> I had hoped that the white moderate would understand that law and order exist for the purpose of establishing justice, and that when they fail to do this they become dangerously structured dams that block the flow of social progress. I had hoped that the white moderate would understand that the present tension of the South is merely a necessary phase from an obnoxious negative peace, where the Negro passively accepted his unjust plight, to a substance-filled positive peace, where all men will respect the dignity and worth of human personality.
>
> (Kramnick and Lowi, 1314)

The more radical form of black liberalism espoused by King and others at mid-century was accompanied by other variations in black political thought, including Black Marxism, Black Nationalism, Pan-Africanism, and Black Conservatism. That the civil rights movement was shaped by each of these political positions speaks to the underlying presence of racial oppression in the United States, which created a nexus of sorts for an elemental black unity – at least with respect to opposition to white supremacy. A number of characters present in Ralph Ellison's *Invisible Man*, published in 1951 – Ras the Exhorter (Black National-ist), Tod Clifton (Black Liberal), and Brother Jack (White Marxist) – present obstacles to black liberation in the novel; this is precisely because their faith is rooted in a specific ideology rather than the fun-damental conceit of liberation (beginning with personal liberation, which, for Ellison, is critical to black, and later human, liberation).

King's Birmingham Letter was written in the year W.E.B. Du Bois died. Du Bois' death announcement was in fact read to the crowd at the March on Washington on December 28, 1963 in Washington, DC. Having traversed both personally and in scholar-ship nearly all forms of black political thought, Du Bois' death marked a closed chapter in black politics. But his first incarnation as a thinker within the liberal political tradition continued to dominate black politics at the time of his death, with organizations like the Southern Christian Leadership Conference (SCLC) and National Association for the Advancement of Colored People (which Du Bois helped to found) at the epicenter of events. But both the strategy and philosophical direction of black liberalism were of necessity informed by forces external to traditional forms of American political thought. More direct action, forceful critiques of inegalitarian fea-tures of American life, and greater claims for economic rights were all critical features of the Black Freedom Struggle, and by the 1960s, even these more moderate perspectives were increasingly dis-ruptive to the American political system.

As leaders of the civil rights movement pushed for more fundamen-tal changes in the American political system, they were perennially challenged to do so with greater force by more left-leaning figures within their own camp. Bayard Rustin, for example, who was a highly influential leader within the movement, was formerly a member of the Communist Party of the United States who had moved to more acceptable forms of socialist ideology. Rustin was also a gay man, a fact that kept much of his advocacy and work within the SCLC in the shadows. It is Rustin, a former Quaker, who is credited in part with informing King's views on pacifism, having travelled to India in 1948. Rustin is purported to have opined:

> I think it's fair to say that Dr. King's view of non-violent tactics was almost non-existent when the [Birmingham] boycott began [in 1956]. In other words, Dr. King was permitting himself and his children and his home to be protected by guns.[12]

Other leaders, including Fannie Lou Hamer, worked in less public roles. Leading a strike of black workers in the Mississippi Delta in 1965, Hamer voiced a radical stance, in support of the strike against white farm owners not paying their black laborers a decent wage. "We got to stop the nervous Nellies and the Toms from going to the Man's place," the *New York Times* reported her commenting at the time. "I don't believe in killing, but a good whipping behind the bushes wouldn't hurt them."[13] As a black woman, Hamer and many other leaders within the movement were forced to play a subordinate role, mimicking the patriarchal structures and practices of the country as a whole. While black political thought countenanced new approaches to resolving age-old forms of inequality within the American political and social system, they often ignored issues of gender equality and empowerment, presuming male leadership and authority as a given.

Notwithstanding these issues of repression within the Black Freedom Struggle, the movement orchestrated a remarkable transformation in American life, including a reconsideration of the underlying ideological beliefs that made white supremacy a "necessity" within American democracy. As the black writer and thinker James Baldwin told the black psychologist Kenneth Clark in a 1963 interview:

> What white people have to do, is to try to find out in their own hearts why it was necessary to have a nigger in the first place, because I'm not a nigger. I'm a man, but if you think I'm a nigger, it means you need it. Why? That's the question you have got to ask yourself – the white population has got to ask itself – north and south – because it's one country for a negro. There's no difference between the north and the south. There's just a difference in the way they castrate you, but the fact of the castration is the American fact. If I'm

not a nigger here, and you, the white people invented him, then you've got to find out why. And the future of the country depends on that. Whether or not it's able to ask that question.

(Standley and Pratt, 45, 1989)

Baldwin's assigned task was formidable, and it may be said to be a work still outstanding; nevertheless, with perhaps the exception of the period encompassing the American Civil War and its aftermath, the civil rights movement (or Black Freedom Struggle) produced unprecedented reevaluations of the American creed – including the creed of white superiority.

From the nineteenth century to the present, one of the chief struggles within black political thought has been between Black Nationalists, who have contended the United States is historically unredeemable as a multiracial democratic project, and Black Liberals, who have argued that it is. This distinction is more fundamental than the more often presented divide over violence and nonviolence as political tactics. Few Black Nationalists have been implicated in political acts of violence against the American state. The crucial ideological divide is what "victory" looks like in the context of racial justice in the United States. For Nationalists such as Martin Delany, Marcus Garvey, and Elijah Muhammad, victory resembled varyingly depicted forms of black independence or autonomy – either in the United States or another country, perhaps in Africa. For Black Liberals, victory most often represented black freedom within a multiracial, democratic United States. Integration, however often presented as the impetus behind the civil rights movement, was never truly an end unto itself; rather, integration was to serve the cause of just socioeconomic and political outcomes – including the right to vote, work, travel, and live without regard to one's racial identity.

By 1967, it was hard to truly distinguish between the political thought of Dr. Martin Luther King, Jr. and Malcolm X, who was assassinated two years earlier. Both King and Malcolm X had moved beyond questions of racial integration – both had come to accept its legitimacy, if not valorization. Both had come to recognize a humanism beyond race and religion; both understood the significance of cultural and aesthetic love for black bodies and personhood; and both had accepted the crucial need for economic development within the African American community. The singular difference was over the question of whether or not nonviolence as a political strategy edified the former necessities for reconstructing black life in America. King never wavered over the question – although he would reason that American violence – the violence of the state – was the foremost evil in the world in need of addressing, rather than black upheaval in the streets. As King said in April of 1967 at Riverside Church in New York:

> As I have walked among the desperate, rejected, and angry young men, I have told them that Molotov cocktails and rifles would not solve their problems. I have tried to offer them my deepest compassion while maintaining my conviction that social change comes most meaningfully through nonviolent action. But they asked, and rightly so, "What about Vietnam?" They asked if our own nation wasn't using massive doses of violence to solve its problems, to bring about the changes it wanted. Their questions hit home, and I knew that I could never again raise my voice against the violence of the oppressed in the ghettos without having first spoken clearly to the greatest purveyor of violence in the world today: my own government.[14]

Having reoriented the discussion of black violence towards the violence of the American state, King placed himself at odds with the traditional liberal tilt of the civil rights movement, the Black Church, the American foreign policy complex, and the presidential administration of Lyndon Johnson. Within one year, he would be assassinated in Memphis, leaving the future of the movement searching for new voices, strategies, and counters to the liberal tradition which had been so central to black political thought and activism.

Racial Fear, Reaction, and the New Federalism

The Black Power movement of the 1960s derided the traditional liberal approach to civil rights. "The major limitation of this approach was that it tended to maintain the traditional dependence of Negroes, and of the movement," said Stokely Carmichael (Kwame Toure) in 1966 (Kramnick and Lowi, 1339). The issue of moving from dependence to black empowerment for Carmichael and other leaders within the Black Panther Party and other new black organizations involved one form of struggle taking place within several other, broader struggles taking place within the American political system.

The New Deal system, itself an assault on laissez-faire liberalism, was now under assault from the right; the civil rights movement was making its own assault on the inflexibility and complicity of the liberal state with American racism; finally, that same civil rights movement was under assault by forces dissatisfied with the gradualism of the movement for Black Liberation. All of these pressures within American politics created instabilities in policies, politics, and social relations, leaving the right and conservatives less vulnerable to questions of governability. As the active force seeking expansion of the powers of the state in American politics, the left, and more specifically the Democratic Party, bore the institutional brunt of dissatisfaction with the system as a whole. The ability to press for the continuation of expansive government programs such as Medicaid and Medicare, coupled with the imperatives of American foreign policy abroad (fighting the Cold War in Vietnam), left the liberal state open to both exogenous and endogenous attacks. The violent political assassinations of John F. Kennedy, Malcolm X, Martin Luther King, Robert F. Kennedy and a host of others rendered shock to the system. The waves of popular uncertainty, unrest, and protest created tremendous space for the reassertion of bedrock American institutions of order: the police, the free market, and the Republican Party.

Alongside these ruptures was perhaps an even more fundamental shift in gender relations, as women asserted new and more radical claims to empowerment. These included not only overtly political rights, but also those related to social relations, including sex, life in the labor force, and in domestic life. As Betty Friedan wrote in *The Feminine Mystique* (1963):

> If I am right, the problem that has no name stirring in the minds of so many American women today is not a matter of loss of femininity or too much education, or the demands of domesticity. It is far more important than anyone recognizes. It is the key to these other new and old problems which have been torturing women and their husbands and children, and puzzling their doctors and educators for years. It may well be the key to the future as

a nation and a culture. We can no longer ignore that voice within women that says: "I want something more than my husband and my children and my home."

(Kramnick and Lowi, 1349)

Friedan's work helped usher in a new set of arguments against an old problem. What was unique was that the timing coincided with transformations taking place in the American workforce since the Second World War – and in technology that made women's control over their bodies and leisure time far less arbitrary.

While much of the feminism of the late 1950s and 1960s was led by, and focused on, middle- and upper-middle-class white women, the general proposition of women's empowerment was broadly asserted as communities of color and working class and poor women claimed their voices within this struggle. As bell hooks would recall over 20 years after the publication of *The Feminine Mystique*, "The bourgeois woman can repudiate family without believing that by doing so she relinquishes the possibility of relationship, care, protection" (Kramnick and Lowi, 1429). In general, assertions against domesticity and traditional sexual and professional mores were deeply disturbing to deeply rooted male power in American life. The pressure to reassert "traditional" values made the candidacy of Richard Nixon in 1968 less of a replay in American politics than a return to social conventions. Nixon's promise to implement "law and order" was in part a response to the overt forces of violent upheaval in American politics; but it was also a directive to stem the tide of the more quiet but equally traumatic forces of change taking place in the United States – namely, the rise of minority rights, women's liberation, and the ongoing push for a reordering of American domestic and foreign policies.

Nixon's electoral victory in 1968 marked a period of Republican Party and conservative resurgence for the next generation. Republicans would go on to win all but one of the five presidential elections between 1968 and 1988, losing the 1976 race in the face of the Watergate scandal and Gerald Ford's pardon of Richard Nixon. While Nixon accommodated a number of liberal programs and established New Deal policies, the general orientation in Washington had changed. The "New Federalism" – formerly known as states' rights – advocated by Nixon and later candidate and President Ronald Reagan sought to empower local governments in the face of massive social upheaval.

The New Federalism was philosophically oriented toward lower taxes, greater corporate power, and the relieving of their tax burden; it also included a new "war" on crime, drugs, and lawlessness, leading to the greatest resurgence in incarceration rates in the nation's history. The Sun Belt policies also sought to move the federal government's attention from the cities to the suburbs, where white flight from urban America had been directed in the aftermath of the upheavals of the 1960s. Civil rights were in and of themselves viewed as a problem, as state attorney generals and the Department of Justice reoriented attention towards "white discrimination" in an attempt to relieve the pressures of litigation against private businesses, universities, and individuals who had formerly pressured to change their discriminatory policies. By 1984, the policies had curried tremendous favor with white voters, with Reagan winning re-election, losing only one state, Democratic Party nominee Walter Mondale's home state of Minnesota.

The formula for winning national elections involved overtly racial arguments for the rejection of the liberal state. As Nicole Mellow has written, "In the 1970s, Republicans encoded race in their attacks on social welfare spending. By the time Ronald Reagan denounced 'welfare queens,' Republicans were regularly using racially charged stereotypes for political and electoral benefit" (Mellow, 42, 2008). For the better part of the 1970s and 1980s, the strategy worked, as demographic strength underlay appeals to white voters, uneasy or otherwise strongly opposed to the radical reappraisal of values that had taken place in the country over the past 30 years.

Conclusion

Historians and political scientists alike have framed the social movements of the mid- to late 1960s as belonging to the "New Left." The premise is fairly simple – an ideology of identities, customs, and opposition to the state arose to challenge the liberalism of government's expansion and provision of social services, along with an all-powerful global military presence. The New Left was, in a sense, the First Left in America – a sociopolitical movement where race, class, gender, and cultural norms were called into question – within the context of a polity highly restrictive of its elite participants and policymakers. Where neo-conservatism was a variation on an earlier premise, the idea of the New Left was reflective of a serious departure from the liberal politics of old.

That Democrats began losing national elections regularly during the rise of this period is suggestive of the natural tendency to seek a scapegoat for political losses; but it also suggests the tendency among liberals to manage questions of identity rather uneasily (where conservatives have historically avoided those questions altogether). This clash among liberals persists to this day – and offers a window into the underlying dominant features of American political thought from the inception: whiteness, maleness, straightness, and property ownership remain the powerfully invisible standard identities. They are "invisible" precisely because they needn't introduce themselves into the public square (unless they are perceived to be "under assault"). The Reagan Era was largely a reassertion of pride in this invisibility – an homage to an earlier time when to be an American meant not having to share something fundamentally different about your person and its representativeness in politics.

Yet between 1988 and 2008, the demographic force of this era began to wane. In 2008, John McCain got nearly the same percentage of the white vote as George H.W. Bush did in his landslide victory of 1988. That McCain, a decorated veteran and prisoner of war, later lost to the nation's first African American president, a man of biracial ancestry and less than direct attachments to the civil rights era, spoke to the newness and inexorable changes taking place within the nation.

In the concluding next chapter, I will highlight the rhetorical and directional similarities between the crucial figures of this pivotal period of change: Ronald Reagan and Barack Obama. There is deep irony in Obama's avowed admiration for Reagan – as deep as Reagan's admiration for FDR, to be sure. But perhaps herein lies a strand of commonality in the American republic and in its political thought. Its ambitions are, in a sense, a core feature of national wisdom – even as its ideas contend within an area happily free from more turbulent political waters.

Notes

1. Commonwealth Club Address, September 23, 1932, transcript, FDR Library. www.fdrlibrary.marist.edu/_resources/images/msf/msf00534.
2. Ibid.

3. Ibid.
4. Ibid.
5. Frances M. Seeber, "Eleanor Roosevelt and Women in the New Deal: A Network of Friends," *Presidential Studies Quarterly*, 20(4), Modern First Ladies White House Organization (Fall), 707–717, 1990.
6. "Anti-Lynching Law, Civil Liberties Unit Sought by Truman," *New York Times*, February 3, 1948.
7. "Battle Against Tradition: Martin Luther King, Jr.," *New York Times*, March 21, 1956.
8. William F. Buckley, Jr., "Our Mission Statement," *The National Review*, November 19, 1955.
9. Ibid.
10. Ibid.
11. William F. Buckley, Jr. "Why the South Must Prevail," *The National Review*, August 24, 1957.
12. Sebastian C. Galbo, "The 'Roving Ambassador': Bayard Rustin's Quaker Cosmopolitanism and the Civil Rights Movement," *Inquiries Journal*, 6(4), 1–4, 2014.
13. "Negro Walkouts in Delta Spurred," *New York Times*, June 7, 1965.
14. https://kinginstitute.stanford.edu/king-papers/documents/beyond-vietnam.

References

Saladin Ambar, *How Governors Built the Modern American Presidency* (Philadelphia, PA: University of Pennsylvania Press, 2012).
Taylor Branch, *Parting the Waters: America in the King Years, 1954–1963* (New York: Simon & Schuster, 1988).
William F. Buckley, Jr., "Our Mission Statement," *The National Review*, November 19, 1955.
William F. Buckley, Jr. "Why the South Must Prevail," *The National Review*, August 24, 1957.
William F. Buckley, Jr., *God and Man at Yale* (Washington, DC: Regnery Publishing, 1986).
Robert A. Caro, *Master of the Senate: The Years of Lyndon Johnson* (New York: Vintage, 2003).
Mary L. Dudziak, *Cold War Civil Rights: Race and the Image of American Democracy* (Princeton, NJ: Princeton University Press, 2000).
Sebastian C. Galbo, "The 'Roving Ambassador': Bayard Rustin's Quaker Cosmopolitanism and the Civil Rights Movement," *Inquiries Journal*, 6(4), 1–4, 2014.
Ira Katznelson, *When Affirmative Action Was White: An Untold History of Racial Inequality in Twentieth-Century America* (New York: W.W. Norton, 2005).

Ira Katznelson, *Fear Itself: The New Deal and the Origins of Our Time* (New York: W.W. Norton, 2013).

Ibram X. Kendi, *Stamped from the Beginning: The Definitive History of Racist Ideas in America* (New York: Nation Books, 2016).

Isaac Kramnick and Theodore Lowi, *American Political Thought: A Norton Anthology* (New York: W.W. Norton, 2009).

William E. Leuchtenburg, *In the Shadow of FDR: From Harry Truman to Barack Obama* (Ithaca, NY: Cornell University Press, 2009).

Kevin J. McMahon, *Reconsidering Roosevelt on Race: How the Presidency Paved the Road to Brown* (Chicago, IL: University of Chicago Press, 2004).

Nicole Mellow, *The State of Disunion: Regional Sources of Modern American Partisanship* (Baltimore, MD: Johns Hopkins University, 2008).

Robert Mickey, *Paths Out of Dixie: The Democratization of Authoritarian Enclaves in America's Deep South, 1944–1972* (Princeton, NJ: Princeton University Press, 2015).

Sidney M. Milkis and Daniel J. Tichenor, *Rivalry and Reform: Presidents, Social Movements, and the Transformation of American Politics* (Chicago, IL: University of Chicago Press, 2019).

Gunnar Myrdal, *An American Dilemma: The Negro Problem and Modern Democracy* (New York: Harper & Brothers, 1944).

Charles J. Ogletree, Jr., *All Deliberate Speed: Reflections on the First Half-Century of Brown v. Board of Education* (New York: W.W. Norton, 2004).

Russell L. Riley, *The Presidency and the Politics of Racial Inequality: Nation-Keeping from 1831–1965* (New York: Columbia University Press, 1999).

Frances M. Seeber, "Eleanor Roosevelt and Women in the New Deal: A Network of Friends," *Presidential Studies Quarterly*, 20(4), Modern First Ladies White House Organization (Fall), 707–717, 1990.

Fred L. Standley and Louis H. Pratt (Eds.), *Conversations with James Baldwin* (Oxford, UK: University Press of Mississippi, 1989).

Brian Stipelman, *That Broader Definition of Liberty: The Theory and Practice of the New Deal* (Lanham, MD: Rowman & Littlefield, 2012).

Garry Wills, *Reagan's America: Innocents at Home* (New York: Penguin Books, 2000).

CHAPTER SEVEN
NEOCONSERVATISM AND SUPERPOWER: 1980–2018

Introduction

Ronald Reagan's political career effectively began in 1964 when he
laid out his conservative political philosophy in what would become
known as "The Speech." In this address, delivered in October, Reagan
expressed his understanding of the American founding and the need
for limited government. What had been a banquet speech honed over
the years working as a spokesman for General Electric, Reagan's talk
would become a popular reference point for conservative values in
Republican circles in the aftermath of the defeat of Senator Barry
Goldwater by Lyndon Johnson in the presidential election of 1964
(Cannon, 125, 2003). "Those who would trade our freedom for the
soup kitchen of the welfare state have told us that they have a utopian
solution of peace without victory," Reagan said, making what would
become a longstanding reference to welfare as an enemy of liberty.[1]

The essential conservative argument against the welfare state was that
it had created a form of dependency among millions of Americans. The
disincentive for work and ambition was evident in the "Great Society"
programs of Lyndon Johnson. But it would take years before Reagan's
message penetrated deeply, most notably in the aftermath of his electoral
victory over Democratic incumbent President Jimmy Carter in 1980.
Unlike Presidents Eisenhower, Nixon, and Ford, Reagan would go on to

make an outright rhetorical and policy-based assault on the New Deal. His victory was a surprise for many liberals. Although the late *New Yorker* film critic Pauline Kael's quote about Richard Nixon's victory has often been connected to Reagan ("I can't believe Nixon won. I don't know anyone who voted for him," she is purported to have said), the point is essentially the same.[2] The line became the impressionistic quip that captured liberalism's elite provincialism among conservatives.

What Reagan represented was an anti-government, pro-business Republican Party conservatism that extended as far back as Calvin Coolidge, and more ambitiously, Alexander Hamilton. This was the traditional form of conservatism that had been largely subordinated to liberalism during the New Deal Era. The turn towards neoconservatism that would shape early twenty-first-century politics and American political thought had more to do with a foreign policy shift that expanded the horizons of what conservatives formerly had opposed on fiscal, if not moral, grounds. While not quite embracing the philosophy of preemptive war that the latter form of conservatism would champion, Reagan nevertheless pushed the envelope with respect to conservative opposition to the Soviet Union, and his Reagan Doctrine attempted to "roll back" rather than contain communist expansion around the world. A similar re-ordering of economic thought with respect to supply-side economics advocated by Reagan marked out the features of a nascent and rebooted conservative policy focus. Indeed, during the primaries in 1980, George H.W. Bush accused Reagan of "voodoo economics" and wanting "to turn the clock back to the eighteenth century."[3] These were attempts to suggest Reagan was out of step with both modernity and traditional Republican Party conservatism. The effort failed, as Reagan won the nomination handily, but it was a potent example of the ascendancy of Reaganism and the intensification of supply-side economics (tax cuts as indispensible to economic growth) within the Republican Party.

In his drubbing of Carter, Reagan lost only Carter's home state of Georgia, in addition to Hawaii, Maryland, Minnesota, West Virginia, and the District of Columbia. The formerly powerful bloc of New Deal voters that had included labor, Catholics, and white ethnics went for Reagan, re-shaping American politics for the next generation. Reagan further secured unity within the Republican Party, choosing Bush as his running mate, bringing the moderate wing of the GOP into the fold – a challenge since Goldwater's defeat in 1964. The difficult unification of the Republican Party was salved by a repudiation of big government seemingly adopted by the populace. As the historian Sean Wilentz has written, "The myths of Reaganism defied American history. From the era of Alexander Hamilton to the era of the Internet, major economic innovation has proceeded in this country with substantial government aid and involvement" (Wilentz, 137, 2008). Voters didn't seem to mind, assessing Jimmy Carter's policies as outworn and ineffective. "Government isn't the solution to our problems," Reagan had warned over and over again. "Government is the problem."[4]

Part of the Reagan "mystique" involved a rewriting of American political history – one FDR and the left had re-written over the preceding 50 years. As the economist Milton Friedman and his co-author and wife Rose Friedman had written:

> A myth has grown up about the United States that paints the nineteenth century as the era of the robber baron, of rugged unrestrained individualism. Heartless monopoly capitalists allegedly exploited the poor, encouraged immigration, and then fleeced the immigrants unmercifully. Wall Street is pictured as conning Main Street, as bleeding the sturdy farmers in the Mid West, who survived despite the widespread distress and misery inflicted on them.
>
> (Kramnick and Lowi, 1425, 2009)

By the Friedmans' sights, there were no robber barons, fleeced immigrants, or heartless monopoly capitalists in the United States of the nineteenth century. Such analyses are reminders that American political thought is about political arguments – about not only the best way to live, but how to see the past. Few if any politicians were as adept as Reagan at giving narration to American history. Not since FDR, who Reagan emulated, was there such a personable chronicler of "the American story."

The conservatives who assumed office in January of 1981 had been out of power for four years – and had not had the kind of anti-government advocate in the White House such as Reagan in their lifetimes. Their political agenda included stemming the tide of civil rights and prioritizing law and order, led by the new Attorney General,

Edwin Meese; reducing taxes on individual households and corporations (led by Friedman); and aggressively challenging Soviet power around the world (led by Defense Secretary Caspar Weinberger). The policy orientation had a number of important successes – as well as significant failures. But the direction of the administration, conservative policymakers, and intellectuals was clear. The vision crystallized by William F. Buckley, Jr. in 1955 with the founding of *The National Review*, had found a home in the White House for the first time in decades, giving hope to conservatives that historical events, marked by government's increased power, would indeed "stop."

Superpower and "The End of History?"

"The end of history will be a very sad time," wrote the political philosopher, Francis Fukuyama, in his highly influential article in 1989, "The End of History?":

> The struggle for recognition, the willingness to risk one's life for a purely abstract goal, the worldwide ideological struggle that called forth daring, courage, imagination, and idealism, will be replaced by economic calculation, the endless solving of technical problems, environmental concerns, and the satisfaction of sophisticated consumer demands.[5]

Fukuyama's twist of triumphal lamentation for the West's victory over communism (and fascism) in the twentieth century, was a byproduct – or so it seemed – of Reaganism's commitment to capitalism and military aggression. "Rolling back" Soviet influence in Latin America, Europe, and the Middle East were all hailed as part of the underlying cause of the Soviet collapse.

Indeed, the Reagan administration risked much, including the presidency itself, in pursuit of challenging communism, as its sale of weapons to Iran in exchange for money routed to the Contras to overthrow the Sandinista government in Nicaragua nearly led to calls for Reagan's impeachment. Yet Fukuyama never mentioned Reagan in his widely touted, and in time equally criticized, article. The end of the Soviet Union was presented as a failure of its ideas – or lack thereof. The ideological drive of Stalinism and its successors was imbued with a statist bent that neglected attention to human freedom and dignity. Fukuyama's article captured the long sought after moment among conservatives when capitalism would hold the ideological field all to itself. For Reagan, his frequent allusions to America as a "shining City upon a hill" was a call to recommit the nation to the kind of exceptionalism that stood with little challenge for decades prior to the Cold War. Reagan ended his Farewell Address to the nation with an allusion to John Winthrop's "City Upon a Hill" speech:

> I've spoken of the shining city all my political life, but I don't know if I ever quite communicated what I saw when I said it. But in my mind, it was a tall proud city built on rocks stronger than oceans, wind swept, God blessed, and teeming with people of all kinds living in harmony and peace – a city with free ports that hummed with commerce and creativity, and if there had to be city walls, the walls had doors, and the doors were open to anyone with the will and the heart to get here.[6]

Reagan's Republican Party would move over time away from the latter portion of this entreaty to welcome outsiders, as its immigration policy began to reflect white voters' unease over the demographic changes afoot in the nation. But for its time, Reagan's political thought was anchored in conservatism newly triumphant – and seemingly unopposed around the world. That confidence was reflected in an iconic advertisement at the close of the twentieth century. The insurance and financial products firm Merrill Lynch commemorated the end of the Cold War and the fall of the Berlin Wall with this statement: "The World is 10 years old. It was born when the Wall fell in 1989."[7] Less than ten years later, Merrill Lynch would declare losses totaling nearly $8 billion as the financial crisis and Great Recession were underway.[8] But in 1999, that seemed a faint possibility. Thomas Paine, who, despite his atheism, Reagan often quoted, once declared: "We have it in our power to make the world over again." That was very much the feeling among conservatives heading into the last decade of the twentieth century.

From 1989 to 1999, the United States enjoyed an unparalleled advantage as the world's sole superpower. And Reagan's largely successful tenure in office did indeed seem to portend the end of a "long twilight struggle" declared by President John F. Kennedy in his Inaugural Address – if not the end of history itself. The United States was varyingly described at home and around the world as a "superpower" or "hyperpower." The fractures of the early twenty-first century were present, but less discussed or worried about. China was experiencing extraordinary economic growth. The United States had experienced two domestic bombings suggestive of an uncertain future – one by a foreign national at the World Trade Center in New York City in 1993; the other by an American citizen in Oklahoma City in 1995 at the Murrah Federal Building. A relatively unknown Russian bureaucrat named Vladimir Putin had become Acting President of Russia on the last day of the decade. While the rise of economic competitors, White Nationalism, and Islamist terror were evident, the 1990s was a period of largely benign, if not farcical, politics. Bill Clinton's presidency was professedly neither liberal nor conservative. It was a "Third Way," as the president proclaimed. In reality, it was a continuation of the rejection of New Deal liberalism, with few exceptions. "The era of big government is over," Bill Clinton declared in his 1996 State of the Union Address."[9] Going into a re-election year, it was a tough sell to liberal Democrats, but Clinton had brought the party victory in 1992, and he read the electorate as still largely in thralldom to Reaganism.

The next presidential election in 2000 between Republican Governor George W. Bush and the Democratic Vice President Al Gore was quickly dubbed a "Seinfeld" election, to cite the then highly popular television series – a "show about nothing" (Davidson, 265, 2016). The line may have captured the last such moment of triumphal, if not banal, politics. The election produced a highly politicized and antagonistic recount, leading to a Supreme Court decision sealing Bush's victory. Before the first year of his administration was over, the United States would face the largest domestic attack on its soil by a foreign adversary in its history; two years later, the nation was at war – not with the nation or citizens who had attacked it, but another, more desirable adversary. That war would not end during Bush's term; it remains a conflict marked by significant losses for American troops, and a brutal occupation leading to hundreds of thousands of deaths and perhaps millions of refugees in the region.[10] This foreign policy disaster was followed up by the worst financial crisis since the Great Depression. All of this seemed a manic reversal of fortunes – an end to the prospect of a happy "boredom" alluded to by Fukuyama at the close of his 1989 article. The first decade of the twenty-first century was anything but boring – and American political thought was compelled to reconsider the nature of conservatism and progressivism alike.

Barack Obama, Progressivism, and the Symbolism of a New Age

During his 2008 campaign for the presidency, Barack Obama, then the Democratic Party nominee, displayed a faux presidential seal at the rostrum at a speech delivered before a group of Democratic governors. The seal contained the phrase "Vero Possumus," or "Yes We Can" in Latin – a loose translation of the candidate's campaign slogan. The seal also had the familiar iconography associated with the Presidential Seal – an eagle clutching arrows along with an olive branch.[11] Some saw the seal as a sign of Obama's arrogance. What was just as likely was an effort on the part of the campaign to surround the nation's first African American presidential nominee with the symbols of presidential power in order to reduce the anxiety on the part of white voters, still unfamiliar with the prospect of being led by a black president. Whatever the reason, the "seal" was short-lived – it was used only for that one event. But it highlighted the divide over Obama and what he represented on either side of the political aisle. On the one hand, he was a visionary leader who would take the nation into a new era of cultural diversity, prosperity, and reasoned leadership. On the other hand, Obama represented the frightening prospect of an identity-driven form of leadership, one whose aspirations were rooted in a desire to "overturn" history – to right the wrongs of white supremacy by reducing whites to a forgotten constituency in this new multicultural landscape.

Neither vision proved accurate. The historian James T. Kloppenberg perhaps captured Obama's moderate progressivism best when, in his study of Obama's political philosophy, he wrote:

> [Obama] has resisted the chorus advising him to portray contemporary politics as a war between good and evil, a morality play in which white-hatted heroes battle black-hatted villains, because that way of framing the issues, at least from his perspective, only intensifies the passions he wants to calm .... Obama has long been a moderate Democrat, a master of mediation drawn toward deliberation rather than drawing lines in the sand.
>
> (Kloppenberg, x, 2012)

The new president's influences ranged from Dr. Martin Luther King, Jr. to the progressives, and finally to the autobiographical narrative of Malcolm X (if not his worldview). In short, Obama is a philosophical pragmatist, Kloppenberg concluded, one whose view of history is informed by incremental progress and a rational dialectic that shapes politics and public policies for the good, over time.[12]

Those on the left and the right interpreted this centrist approach married to a progressive philosophy in more radical terms. For conservatives, Obama was a radical pro-government ideologue whose internationalism and cultural cosmopolitanism made him essentially un-American – or at a minimum, outside the mainstream of the American political tradition. This was not an entirely new depiction of Democratic presidents. What were new were the racialist attachments to criticisms of Obama – and those married to his background as someone familiar with the Islamic world. These made Obama varyingly "Islamist," "Muslim," or "Kenyan." On occasion, it made him all of these at once.

For many progressives, Obama was too centrist, too accommodating of racial injustice and a militarist American foreign policy. Weeks after his election, Cornel West reflected on Obama's early cabinet picks, critiquing them as a byproduct of someone "who wants to govern as a liberal centrist."[13] The critique, one that would later become identified with more personal attacks, reflected a challenge within black and progressive political thought in the country. The masses of African Americans were, and remained, overwhelmingly supportive of Obama and his presidency, while many on the left, including black intellectuals and activists, were dismayed. The democratic impulse to side with the people put Obama's critics in a difficult position, an elitist stance seemingly out of lock-step with the people whose interests they were seeking to represent.

Had Obama's election heralded a post-Reagan, if not post-racial, America, as West and others had hoped? Or was Obama's reticence to take bolder action as president a pragmatic approach to governing in a country still very much enamored by Reaganism and conservative political philosophy? The structural impediments to a more progressive Obama presidency included those deeply rooted in constitutional reality – a Senate that exaggerated the influence of smaller, whiter, and less progressive states, and a conservative majority on the Supreme Court. In addition, Obama faced the scrutiny of establishing precedents in ways not entirely unlike Washington. His every action – both personal and political – would be viewed within the context of his blackness, and in effect, the ability, if not propriety, of African Americans governing at the presidential level. In a sense, Obama's presidency put both his supporters and detractors on the left in a precarious position. The only clear path was one of resistance, one utilized to great effect by his Republican opponents. In his Inaugural, Obama attempted to marry the progressive politics of the early twentieth century with the center-right politics of his era. Extolling a politics of responsibility, his calls for a renewal of civic republicanism were difficult to oppose, but perhaps equally difficult to arouse great enthusiasm:

> What is required of us now is a new era of responsibility – a recognition on the part of every American that we have duties to ourselves, our nation and the world; duties that we do not grudgingly accept, but rather seize gladly, firm in the knowledge that there is nothing so satisfying to the spirit, so defining of our character than giving our all to a difficult task. This is the price and the promise of citizenship.[14]

In this address, Obama praised market forces while promising to rein them in; he argued not for a big or small government, but one that worked; and he promised a foreign policy that would neither abandon American ideals nor its national security interests. In short, it was a speech designed to hold the center, rather than one seeking to articulate a clearly progressive path. The pageantry of the moment, with perhaps over a million onlookers at the Mall in Washington, and the First Family resplendent and beaming throughout, captured the imagination (and undoubtedly the fears) of many. From the vantage point of American political thought, however, the moment – at least rhetorically – heralded only the slightest of cracks in the edifice of Reaganism. It was hardly the chasm some had hoped for.

Barack Obama's Presidency: Neoconservative and Neoliberal Pathways

Barack Obama was a State senator in Illinois when the United States Senate voted in favor of authorizing the President of the United States

George Bush to take the nation to war in Iraq in October of 2002. The resolution was very broad, authorizing President George W. Bush "to use the Armed Forces of the United States as he determines to be necessary and appropriate in order to defend the national security of the United States against the continuing threat posed by Iraq."[15] The breadth of the authorization was presumed to grant authority for Bush to use so-called tactical nuclear weapons if necessary. No Democratic candidates for the presidency in 2008 opposed the resolution. Obama, spoke out against it at the time, but had no vote, and was barely known outside of his home state at the time.

The United States war in Iraq was the culmination of the rise of the neoconservative movement – a philosophy rooted in pressing for America to use its unprecedented status as a superpower in a "unipolar" world to advance democracy. Conservatism's modern 100-year history had thus moved from an early period of anti-war and anti-internationalist positions to an internationalist containment policy, later accompanied by a rollback agenda for diminishing Soviet power globally; the Second Iraq War challenged conservatism's premise in the "War on Terror," making the shift to fighting preemptive wars. This position was at the heart of neoconservative claims, including those made by Bush's Secretary of Defense Donald Rumsfeld, his Vice President Dick Cheney, and his Deputy Secretary of Defense Paul Wolfowitz. Bush's decision to take the nation to war preemptively against a nation that had not attacked the United States, without evidence of "weapons of mass destruction," was contested in the form of national protests, but few in Washington challenged it in the aftermath of the attacks on the country on September 11, 2001. Vice President Chaney was reported to have argued in November of 2001 "that if there was a one percent chance that a threat was real, [the United States] would have to treat it as if it were a certainty in terms of our response."[16] This doctrine later won the favor of the old-line conservatives in the Bush White House, including Secretary of State Colin Powell, who, despite internal policy debates and protests, became the face of the administration in advancing claims of weapons of mass destruction against Iraq before the United Nations.

Barack Obama's opposition to the war gave him an immediate pathway to the Democratic Party nomination in 2008, albeit a slim one. Proving to be an effective campaigner, and seeking to unite the country in the aftermath of the war's unsuccessful turn, Obama attempted to steer a pragmatic path, meeting very early on with conservative intellectuals days before his inauguration, hoping to carve out a middle path of sorts.[17] Such a path included appointing key figures from the moderate wing of the Democratic Party, including Joe Biden as his Vice President, and his rival for the nomination, Hillary Clinton, as Secretary of State. Obama's opposition to the war was rooted in a formal respect for America's foreign policy tradition, one opposed to preemptive wars, if not preemptive (covert) interventions. From a policy standpoint, this was in keeping with American political history, as there had been no American "left" historically represented in the nation's foreign policy apparatus. From Woodrow Wilson forward, American liberal foreign policy leadership reflected an internationalist, interventionist, and corporatist predisposition. Barack Obama's presidency was no different, only eschewing the neoconservative grafting of preemptive war onto this set of prerogatives.

Obama's signature domestic policy initiative was his health care proposal. Despite being made up of components largely culled from Republican ideas put forth in the 1990s, the Affordable Care Act drew no congressional support from Republicans. Obama's congeniality, centrism, and politics of respectability could not overcome the symbolic danger his presidency posed for many whites in the Republican electorate who viewed him with deep suspicion – and outright cases of mistaken identity. Over 40 percent of registered Republicans presumed him to be Muslim.[18] Few in the party, aside from former Secretary of State Colin Powell, bothered to ask, "What would be wrong if he were?"[19]

Obama used a great deal of his political capital in pushing for passage of the Affordable Care Act – invoking Lincoln in a closed session with House Democrats before the historic vote:

> I have the great pleasure of having a really nice library at the White House. And I was tooling through some of the writings of some previous Presidents and I came upon this quote by Abraham Lincoln: "I am not bound to win, but I'm bound to be true. I'm not bound to succeed, but I'm bound to live up to what light I have."[20]

As the political scientist John J. Pitney, Jr. reported at the time, Lincoln apparently never uttered or wrote these words. But Obama's attribution – whether it came from his library or not – suggests the president sought a connection to the Great Emancipator in this legislation – an effort to place the capstone on the achievements of the New Deal and

Great Society that only a great executive could achieve. The law proved to go through a period of great unpopularity, followed by a climb in the polls in terms of its favorability, where a majority of the American public now view it favorably – including a good many Republicans.

With the Supreme Court upholding the constitutionality of the Act, Obama's chief legislative achievement has stood for ten years now. That success suggests something about the aspirations of America's liberal party in recent decades; holding the line on a formerly right-of-center policy proposal constitutes great victory where the electorate may be more disposed to progressive policies, but where the mechanisms of Madisonian democracy favor veto power and exaggerated influence in the Senate and Supreme Court. Progressive politics is increasingly difficult, and the racial additive of support for an African American president undoubtedly complicated matters that otherwise would have played out along strictly policy lines.

The racial demographics of recent decades have shaped the nature of American politics in ways social scientists and historians are still coming to terms with. In a crushing electoral defeat, George H.W. Bush won 60 percent of the white vote in his resounding defeat of Democrat Michael Dukakis. By 2012, Republican Mitt Romney would nearly match Bush, winning 59 percent of the white vote; but he would lose the election to Barack Obama, who would garner a comfortable, if not historic, margin in the Electoral College.[21] Within a generation, the white vote in presidential elections would not prove predictive for the Republican Party. How this would shape American politics and the direction of American political thought was a question we are only now coming to terms with.

White Nationalism, Populism, and the Rise of Trumpism in American Politics

In the wake of Donald Trump's election to the presidency in 2016, the political scientists Philip A. Klinkner and Rogers Smith reminded Americans, "the U.S. has always had at least one (and often more than one) major political party devoted to some notion of white nationalism."[22] In focusing on the Know Nothings, for example, Americans have often presumed that the Democratic and Republican Parties have been varyingly (white) nationalist. What was new about the Trump campaign and early presidency was that there had not been an overtly white nationalist president in modern American history. As he said at a campaign rally before the 2018 midterm elections:

> A globalist is a person that wants the globe to do well, frankly, not caring about our country so much. And you know what? We can't have that .... You know, they have a word – it's sort of became old-fashioned – it's called a "nationalist." And I say, really, we're not supposed to use that word. You know what I am? I'm a nationalist, okay? I'm a nationalist. Nationalist. Nothing wrong. Use that word. Use that word.[23]

Trump's reference to the opprobrium attached to the term suggests he, or his advisers, understood its connection with racism and white supremacy. That he used it anyway reflects a comfort with the political thought of white nationalism that transcends ordinary politics.

Trump's election was the product of electoral victory in an amalgam of key formerly reliably Democratic and post-industrial states: Pennsylvania, Michigan, and Wisconsin. He defeated the Democratic nominee Hillary Clinton by a margin of fewer than 80,000 votes in these three states. Running on an anti-immigrant and anti-globalist message, Trump's message resonated with many white voters who felt the post-industrial, free-trade agenda of Washington over recent decades no longer spoke to their interests. Both his and Bernie Sanders' (Independent-VT) success in the respective Republican and Democratic Party primaries, despite the otherwise wide divide in their political messages, spoke to both the conservative and neoliberal failure to address economic inequality and the plight of the working class in America. Trump's visceral attacks on immigrants – especially Mexicans and Muslims – antagonized many, while also inspiring a critical segment of his supporters. The Trump–Sanders hold on the electorate, however ironic the pairing of a life-long industrial capitalist and xenophobe, and a life-long Democratic Socialist, was reminiscent of at least one aspect of the 1968 presidential primaries, where many voters claimed a willingness to vote either for Robert F. Kennedy or George Wallace (Clarke, 4–5, 2008).

Trump's appeal to the white working class reflected a number of concerns and fears of that part of the electorate: the loss and irreplaceable nature of certain industrial jobs; the rise of racial minorities in America;

and finally, the fear of Muslim communities in the United States and their purported ties to Islamic extremism around the world. In each case, Trump's brand of populism and effective use of the media won him solid, if not majority, support among Republicans, and later, among the broader swath of Americans. By the summer of 2019, he still had not recorded a Gallup poll placing him at or above 50 percent approval.[24]

Given a more robust economy with jobless numbers down to near historic lows, Trump's inability to gain greater support reflected poorly on this form of populism's ability to govern successfully. The underlying political thought of Trump's appeal has been rather dark – certainly by American presidential standards of rhetoric. The Inaugural Address, in this respect, was especially bleak:

> [F]or too many of our citizens, a different reality exists: Mothers and children trapped in poverty in our inner cities; rusted-out factories scattered like tombstones across the landscape of our nation; an education system, flush with cash, but which leaves our young and beautiful students deprived of knowledge; and the crime and gangs and drugs that have stolen too many lives and robbed our country of so much unrealized potential. This American carnage stops right here and stops right now.[25]

It was an odd turn of phrase – "American carnage" – one that went beyond any previous rhetorical flourishes in the nation's political history. Neither Jimmy Carter's "malaise" speech (a word never uttered in his "Crisis of Confidence" address in the Oval Office) nor John F. Kennedy's "long twilight struggle" (about the Cold War) quite captured Trump's depiction of the United States at the brink of something quite so troubling. But the entirety of Trump's appeal was that somehow over the past eight years or more the "greatness" of America had been dislodged and was in need of restoration. Political observers could be forgiven if they were less than surprised at the turn of events envisioned by Trump as the early re-election season got underway. Somehow, the carnage had been removed within a two-year period, and a new campaign slogan – "Keep America Great" – was deployed. Never one to avoid telegraphing his intent, the president sought the opinion of the crowd at an early campaign rally. "It's hard. It's the greatest theme in the history of American politics," Trump mused. "How do you give that up for a new one?"[26]

In the end, "Keep America Great" won out. The carnage was officially over.

Presidential historians have generally regarded Franklin Roosevelt and Ronald Reagan as the strongest pitchmen in modern American politics. Trump is something more – and less. His vision is less concerned about selling the country on a particular policy, or even policy direction. The president remains the ultimate product, and his victory *is* the national achievement. This is not so much the end of conservatism as much as it is the end of ideology – at least in presidential politics. The ideological direction of the nation – the *thought* within American political thought – is shaped by others in the present administration. It is hard to discern, though wary Republicans point to federal judges and Supreme Court Justices the president has successfully nominated and advanced.

With the two-year-long Mueller Investigation concluding that the president could not be found to have engaged in a provable conspiracy involving electoral interference from Russia nor finding enough exculpatory evidence to exonerate him from obstruction of justice, the nation was left to ponder what had happened – and how those who had engaged in wrongdoing would be punished. While some key figures were convicted and ultimately sentenced, the findings seemed anticlimactic. That is perhaps the best word, one often associated with television and the world of make believe, to describe the results of those democratic forces at play in an effort to adjudicate what happened in the election of 2016.

Conclusion: Surf against the Sides, Boats against the Current

Superpower. Inverted totalitarianism. Fugitive democracy. These were all terms the great American political theorist Sheldon Wolin applied to democratic conditions in the United States in 2004 (Wolin, 2004). The first, "superpower," refers to Plato's theory of regime change, where democracy degenerates into tyranny, becoming one of its supportive elements (Wolin, 585). The second, "inverted totalitarianism," is defined by a government that "controls, punishes, surveys, directs, and influences" citizens while simultaneously fragmenting potential citizen opposition along racial, gendered, ethnic, and sexual lines (Wolin, xvi) Finally, "fugitive democracy" was Wolin's expression for democracy's "protean and amorphous" nature. "I have called it 'fugitive democracy' in order to emphasize its necessarily occasional character," he wrote (Wolin, 602).

Wolin's significance as a writer and teacher in the second half of the twentieth century underscored the gravity of his conclusions. Of course, his expanded edition of *Politics and Vision*, originally released in 1960, was published in 2004, at the height of controversy surrounding America's intervention and conduct during the Second Persian Gulf War, fought in Iraq. Now, some 15 years later, with neo-conservatism largely in disrepute, even for the Republican president, the contemporary challenge to American democracy cannot be confined to a single ideology. The amalgam of conservatism, liberalism, neoliberalism, neoconservatism, nationalism, and populism all have suffered from a continuity of an underlying will to power checked on occasion by the republican impulses of community, virtue, fairness, and equality. These countervailing impulses have been all the more readily dismissed or countered by accusations of their "special pleading" for particular groups: women, African Americans, Latinos, Asians, Muslim and Middle Eastern and North African communities, gays and queer-identifying Americans, and indigenous peoples.

In short, there has been no dominant American political thought, past or present, that has not succumbed to, in some form or fashion, the desire for a restrictive democratic system. As Michael Hanchard has pointed out, this is not new to the American democratic experience, but rather a historic phenomenon as old as democracy itself (Hanchard, 2018). This places the future of American political thought at a crossroads, as disenfranchised or marginalized communities hold its racialized and patriarchal tendencies in contempt, while conservative, nationalist, and populist-inspired elites and voters regard it as increasingly restrictive of more avowedly racialist objectives. Given that American political thought must hold democratic inquiry and processes in esteem, this poses difficulties where formerly majority communities become minorities, and the racial demography of the nation shifts the political rewards of society from those who have held a form of monopoly on its power.

In *Politics and Vision*, Wolin alluded to the increasing role culture would play, and was already playing, in articulating democratic visions. "In some quarters," Wolin wrote, "the shift to cultural politics is buoyed by the belief that to interpret culture radically is the means of changing a changing world" (Wolin, 581). Taking Wolin at his word, this is at once an assertion and a concession. The assertion has to do with culture's power to inspire and transform society through forms of subversion that speak to human needs that are, strictly speaking, apolitical – these include love, desire, friendship, beauty, and contemplation. The concession has to do with the recognition that our present politics serves only the most ephemeral of interests well – corporations, shareholders, and the powerful – while remaining at loggerheads over almost anything to do with the public interest broadly defined.

The American literary tradition has always played an outsized role in shaping, embellishing, and oftentimes widening the direction of American political thought. In a country whose philosophy's most original contribution may be said to be one that stands outside of philosophy – and by this, I am referring to pragmatism – we are engaging in a field necessarily tightly bound. For this reason, we must look to Poe, Hawthorne, Melville, Dickinson, Jackson, Plath, Wright, Hurston, Baldwin, and Morrison, among the rich pantheon of thinkers whose work fills in the space American philosophy has *evaded*, to employ the word Cornel West used to describe the American experience with the discipline of philosophy (West, 1989).

As West's work argues, such an evasion is not inherently troubling, if it presupposes an engagement with real-world problems found in the body politic. By moving to the American literary tradition (or the realm of the visual or performing arts, for that matter), writers from Harold Bloom to Toni Morrison have called upon us to examine the genius of American political thought, wherever it may be found. Characters in Jonathan Franzen's novel *Freedom* (2010), for example, encounter the uniquely American problem of "how to live." Surely, this isn't unique to the American experience? Yet the expressed intent of happiness imposed by Jefferson on the democratic experiment has created both national and personal embarrassment. For the former, it is for the unhappiness attendant to all manners of inequality historically; for the latter, it is found in the embarrassment of unhappiness found in perpetual longing, an essential development in a commercial republic. Franzen's novel has been called the first great American novel of the new century. But its theme is old and worn:

How to live?[27]

"I'm sorry," he said, "I'm still trying to figure out how to live."[28]

However little he'd ever known how to live, he'd never known less than he'd known now.[29]

For Franzen, freedom is paralyzing in a society whose politics is rooted in the expectation of happiness. It is therefore naturally all the more devastating to those who have ever been on the margins of even holding such expectations. In this sense, who has been freer than African Americans? "I heard a Negro the other day say 'our astronauts,'" Malcolm X said sardonically in his "Message to the Grassroots" in 1963. "Imagine … 'Our astronauts.' They won't even let him near that plant. That's a Negro that's out of his mind" (Malcolm X, 12, 1965).

There is powerful liberty in not fooling oneself, a difficult disposition to adopt under most any circumstance – all the more so in the United States, where hope is at once an eternal political slogan and national ethos. It therefore makes sense that perhaps the two greatest novels in American history, *Moby-Dick* and *The Great Gatsby*, end on the same note: a relentless push into the past, despite our best efforts to move forward:

> Now small fowls flew screaming over the yet yawning gulf; a sullen white surf beat against its steep sides; then all collapsed, and the great shroud of the sea rolled on as it rolled five thousand years ago.
>
> (Melville, 1407, 1983)

> So we beat on, boats against the current, borne back ceaselessly into the past.
>
> (Fitzgerald, 180, 1953)

The American democratic experiment, like the thought that emanates from it, compels its citizens to wage a perpetual struggle against what has been and what might be. It is found in the long hyphen at the end of Robert Frost's "The Road Not Taken," or the transition at two minutes in the middle of Jimi Hendrix's note-bending rendition of Bob Dylan's "All Along the Watchtower." Something has happened – is happening; and as we seek to impose our will on the past, *we* change. And perhaps, a new past – for those unborn – is created.

Notes

1. Ronald Reagan, "Goldwater Campaign Speech," reprinted in the *Los Angeles Times*, June 21, 2001.
2. www.commentarymagazine.com/politics-ideas/acceptable-polite-society/.
3. "George Bush Running Hard, with Brand New Track Suit," *New York Times*, April 27, 1980.
4. "Reagan's Dramatic Success," *New York Times*, January 21, 1981.
5. Francis Fukuyama, "The End of History?" *The National Interest* (Summer), 3–18, 1989.
6. "Transcript of Reagan's Farewell Address to the American People," *New York Times*, January 12, 1989.
7. www.adforum.com/creative-work/ad/player/15812/the-world-is-10-years-old/merrill-lynch.
8. www.forbes.com/sites/katestalter/2017/10/24/the-demise-of-merrill-lynch-revisiting-its-monumental-write-down-10-years-ago/#2d328d0e53bb.
9. https://clintonwhitehouse4.archives.gov/WH/New/other/sotu.html.
10. "15 Years after the Iraq War Began, the Death Toll Is Still Murky," *Washington Post*, March 20, 2018.
11. "The Great Seal of Obamaland?" *New York Times*, June 20, 2008.
12. "In Writings of Obama, a Philosophy Is Unearthed," *New York Times*, October 27, 2010.
13. www.democracynow.org/2008/11/19/cornel_west_on_the_election_of.
14. https://obamawhitehouse.archives.gov/blog/2009/01/21/president-barack-obamas-inaugural-address.
15. https://georgewbush-whitehouse.archives.gov/news/releases/2002/10/20021002-2.html.
16. www.newyorker.com/magazine/2006/07/03/the-one-percent-doctrine.
17. http://voices.washingtonpost.com/44/2009/01/obama-pulls-up-a-chair-at-geor.html.
18. https://thehill.com/blogs/blog-briefing-room/news/253515-poll-43-percent-of-republicans-believe-obama-is-a-muslim.
19. www.politico.com/blogs/jonathanmartin/1008/Powell_embarrased_by_the_ObamaisaMuslim_stuff.html.
20. www.npr.org/templates/story/story.php?storyId=125169095.
21. https://ropercenter.cornell.edu/how-groups-voted-2012.
22. "Trump's Election Is Actually a Return to Normal Racial Politics. Here's Why," *Washington Post*, November 17, 2016.
23. "Trump's Use of a Fraught Term – 'Nationalist' – Could Cement a Dangerous Racial Divide," *Washington Post*, October 23, 2018.
24. https://news.gallup.com/poll/203207/trump-job-approval-weekly.aspx.

25. www.whitehouse.gov/briefings-statements/the-inaugural-address/.
26. "In Reelection Pitch, Trump Seeks to Balance Grievance and Accomplishment," *Los Angeles Times,* April 28, 2019.
27. Jonathan Franzen, *Freedom* (New York: Farrar, Straus, and Giroux, 2010), 319.
28. Ibid., 336.
29. Ibid., 557.

References

Lou Cannon, *Governor Reagan: His Rise to Power* (New York: Public Affairs, 2003).

Thurston Clarke, *The Last Campaign: Robert F. Kennedy and 82 Days that Inspired America* (New York: Henry Holt, 2008).

Telly Davidson, *Culture War: How the '90s Made Us Who We Are Today Whether We Like It or Not* (Jefferson, NC: McFarland, 2016).

F. Scott Fitzgerald, *The Great Gatsby* (New York: Scribner, 1953).

Jonathan Franzen, *Freedom* (New York: Farrar, Straus, and Giroux, 2010).

Francis Fukuyama, "The End of History?" *The National Interest* (Summer), 3–18, 1989.

Michael Hanchard, *The Spectre of Race: How Discrimination Haunts Western Democracy* (Princeton, NJ: Princeton University Press, 2018).

James T. Kloppenberg, *Reading Obama: Dreams, Hope, and the American Political Tradition* (Princeton, NJ: Princeton University Press, 2012).

Isaac Kramnick and Theodore J. Lowi, *American Political Thought: A Norton Anthology* (New York: W.W. Norton, 2009).

Herman Melville, *Herman Melville: Redburn, White-Jacket, Moby Dick* (New York: Library of America, 1983).

Cornel West, *The American Evasion of Philosophy: A Genealogy of Pragmatism* (Madison, WI: University of Wisconsin Press, 1989).

Sean Wilentz, *The Age of Reagan: A History, 1974–2008* (New York: Harper-Collins, 2008).

Sheldon Wolin, *Politics and Vision: Continuity and Innovation in Western Political Thought* (Princeton, NJ: Princeton University Press, 2004).

Malcolm X, *Malcolm X Speaks* (George Breitman, Ed.) (New York: Grove Press, 1965).

INDEX

9/11 97, 154, 158
14th Amendment of the American Constitution 98, 99, 132
15th Amendment of the American Constitution 69
19th Amendment of the American Constitution 112, 113
1491: New Revelations of the Americas before Columbus (Mann) 14

A

abolitionist movement 60, 63, 66, 69, 74, 80–81, 89, 90
Adams, Abigail 66
Adams, John 27, 32, 42, 44, 49, 66
Addams, Jane 120
administration, development of 103–104
Affordable Care Act 159–160
African Americans 166; exclusion under New Deal policies 128, 129–130; and the Obama presidency 156, 157; Progressive era 120–121; and rights in the 1932–1980 period 128–129, 131–134, 135, 136–141; *see also* blacks
African slavery *see* slavery
Alien and Sedition Acts 44, 45, 47

"All Along the Watchtower" (Hendrix) 166
American bicentennial 35
American Constitution 9–10, 11, 86; 14th Amendment 98, 99, 132; 15th Amendment 69; 19th Amendment 112, 113; Article II 43–44; and gender 41; political thought of 38–42
American exceptionalism 18–19, 28, 79, 100
American literature 3–4, 165
American Revolution period 9–10, 31–32, 48–49; American Constitution, political thought of 38–42; and the Articles of Confederation 36–38; Jefferson presidency 45–48; national identity, forging of 42–45; and race 32, 33–36, 40–41, 46–47, 48
Anglo-Saxons 107
Anti-Federalists 36, 39, 40, 59
anti-lynching legislation 131
Appiah, Kwame Anthony 106
Arendt, Hannah 27, 31–32, 126
armed forces, desegregation of 131, 132
Art of Virtue, The (Franklin) 25
Article II of the American Constitution 43–44
Articles of Confederation 10, 36–38, 58, 75
Asian Americans 108, 109

B

Babb, Valerie 14–15, 70
Babe Ruth 94
Bacon's Rebellion, 1676 21
Baldwin, James 139–140
Balogh, Brian 112
Barbary Coast, North Africa, war 46
"Bartleby the Scrivener: A Tale of Wall
   Street" (Melville) 104–105, 121
Battle-Pieces and Aspects of the War
   (Melville) 93
Beloved (Morrison) 115
Benhabib, Seyla 3
Benito Cereno (Melville) 85
Bensel, Richard 4, 103
Berle, Adolf A. 125, 127
Bernasconi, Robert 25
Biden, Joe 159
Bill of Rights 98
Black Conservatism 138
Black Freedom Struggle 7, 95, 132, 136,
   138, 139–140
Black Hawk War, 1832 70
Black Liberals 140
Black Liberation 142
Black Marxism 138
Black Nationalism 138, 140
Black Panther Party 28, 34, 142
Black Power movement 141–142
Black Skin, White Masks (Fanon) 64
black women: American Revolution
   period 41; and the civil rights
   movement 139; and exclusion under
   New Deal policies 129; racial
   oppression of 67, 69; suffrage and
   political rights 112–113; *see also*
   white women; women
Blackburn, Robin 58
blacks: and employment 111; and
   positionality of book 3; racial sex/
   marriage laws in colonial period 22;
   suffrage and political rights 69; *see
   also* African Americans; slavery
Bloom, Harold 81, 165
"blowback" concept in foreign policy 97
Borneman, Walter R. 26
Brown, John 90

Brown v. Board of Education (1954) 108,
   128, 132, 133
Buchanan, James 85
Buckley, William F. 28, 34, 134,
   135–136, 152
Burlingame, Michael 35
Burr, Aaron 57
Bush, George H.W. 145, 150–151, 160
Bush, George W. 97, 154, 158

C

Calhoun, John C. 59, 62, 65
California 74, 85
capitalism 84, 119, 130
Capitalism and Slavery (Williams) 20
Carmichael, Stokely 141–142
Carter, Jimmy 149, 150, 151, 162
Catholicism 109
Ceaser, James W. 10
Cheney, Dick 158
Cherokee people 70
Chestnut, Mary 91
Chickasaw people 70
China 154
Chinese immigrants 108, 109, 110;
   Chinese Exclusion Act, 1882 7, 108,
   109
Choctaw people 70
Christian crusader wars 17
"Christian at His Calling, A." (Mather) 15
"City Upon a Hill" speech ("A Modell of
   Christian Charity") (Winthrop) 17,
   153
civil disobedience 55, 105
civil rights 131–134, 137–141, 144; and
   neoconservatism 151–152; *see also*
   Black Freedom Struggle
Civil Rights Act 131
Civil War and Reconstruction period 7,
   79–82, 98–100; and Lincoln 80, 83,
   87, 88, 90–91, 92–93, 93–98, 99,
   100; race and slavery 80–81, 82–89,
   90–91, 92, 93, 95, 97, 98, 99, 100;
   violence and liberal politics 89–93
Clark, Kenneth 139–140
Clay, Henry 60, 84
Clinton, Bill 154

Clinton, Hillary 159, 161
Coates, Ta-Nehisi 98
Cobb, Josephine 93–94
Cold War 118, 130, 153; *see also* Soviet
    Union
colonial period and legacy 6, 9–12,
    27–28; indigenous history and New
    Eden myth 12–16; origins of colonial
    thought 16–20; political though to
    French and Indian War 24–27;
    slavery 6, 10, 11, 20–24
commercial republic, America as 80
Committee on Civil Rights 131
Commonwealth Club Address (F.D.
    Roosevelt) 125, 126–127
communism 130, 152
Compromise of 1850 60, 73–74,
    81, 84
Compromise of 1877 82, 84, 100
Congress 40, 60, 83
Conscience of a Conservative, The
    (Goldwater) 136
conservatism: late twentieth century
    149–150; mid-twentieth century
    134–137; *see also* neoconservatism
Constitutional Convention 36, 38, 40,
    41, 43, 80, 83
Coolidge, Calvin 150
Cooper, James Fennimore 27, 56, 71
Cooper, John Milton 118
Creek people 70
Croly, Herbert 119
Cruse, Harold 4
Cuba 117
cultural politics 164–165

D

Davis, Jefferson 92
Declaration of Independence 10, 11, 32,
    34, 35, 36, 40, 45, 61, 66, 74, 81,
    86, 94
Delany, Martin 140
Democracy in America (Tocqueville)
    10–12, 23, 36, 54, 64–65, 104
Democratic Party 59, 126, 131, 132, 136,
    142, 145, 159, 160
Democratic Republicans 47

desegregation 133; of armed forces
    131, 132; of education 108, 128,
    132, 133; *see also* racial segregation
Dewey, John 120, 121
Dickinson, John 27
Dixiecrats 132
Douglas, Stephen 88, 89
Douglass, Frederick 65, 69, 90, 111
Dred Scott case 74, 82, 86–87, 90, 91
Du Bois, W.E.B. 12, 106–107, 113, 117,
    120, 138
Duane, James 37
Dudziak, Mary L. 131–132
Dukakis, Michael 160
Dunbar-Ortiz, Roxanne 14
Dylan, Bob 4, 166

E

Eastern European immigrants 110
Eastland, James O. 131
education: desegregation of 108, 128,
    132, 133
Edwards, Rebecca 92
Eisenhower, D. 132, 133, 136, 149
Ellison, Ralph 2, 21, 85, 138
Emancipation Proclamation 93, 133
Emerson, Ralph Waldo 4, 25, 54, 60, 71
"Empire of Liberty" period 53–57,
    73–74; 1800 election, and beyond
    57–61; black rebellion and racial
    order 61–65; settlement nation 70–73;
    suffrage and citizenship 65–70
"End of History, The" (Fukuyama)
    152–153, 154–155
England: colonization of Ireland 17;
    English identity in the colonial
    period 16
Enlightenment 10, 23–24, 25, 28, 32
"Era of Good Feelings" 59
Espionage and Sedition Acts 118
eugenics 110

F

Fanon, Franz 64
Farewell Address (Reagan) 153

Federalist Papers/The Federalist 9–10, 39–40, 43, 94
Federalists 40, 42, 46, 47, 53, 58
Feminine Mystique, The (Friedan) 142–143
feminism 143; *see also* gender; women
Ferguson, Bob 117
financial crisis, 2008 153, 154
First World War 114, 117–118, 120
Fitzgerald, F. Scott 12–13, 14, 22, 24, 110, 121, 122, 166
Foner, Eric 63, 80, 84, 86, 90, 91, 100
Ford, Gerald 149
foreign policy: George W. Bush 154, 158; and neoconservatism 150
"forgetting" 9, 10, 23
Fort Sumner 92
Forten, James 81
"Founding Fathers" 38
Framers of the Constitution 32, 36, 39, 87, 89
Franklin, Benjamin 24–25, 41
Franzen, Jonathan 165–166
Freedom (Franzen) 165–166
Freikorps, Germany 117
French and Indian War 26, 56, 89
French Revolution 31, 47
Friedan, Betty 142–143
Friedman, Milton 151
Friedman, Rose 151
Frost, Robert 4, 166
Frymer, Paul 38, 45, 48, 91–92, 93, 99
"fugitive democracy" 163
Fugitive Slave Act 40, 66, 71, 74
Fukuyama, Francis 152–153, 154–155
Fuller, Margaret 60–61

G

Gage, Frances Dana 66
Garvey, Marcus 140
gender: American Revolution period 32, 41, 47; and the Articles of Confederation 37; and the Declaration of Independence 35; "Empire of Liberty" period 60–61, 65–70, 71–72; positionality of book 2, 3, 6; and presidencies 41; and

rights in the 1932–1980 period 142–143; *see also* women
George III, King 33, 34, 61
Georgetown University 2, 4
German immigrants 109
Gettysburg Address 10, 38, 40, 82, 86, 94–95, 96–97, 98, 100
Gienapp, William 80, 83, 94, 95, 96, 97
God and Man at Yale (Buckley) 135, 136
Goldwater, Barry 136, 149, 151
Good Master Well Served, A. (Mather) 22–23
Gopnik, Adam 92
Gore, Al 154
Graff, Jacob 33
Grant, Ulysses S. 93
Great Depression 121, 126, 127
Great Gatsby, The (Fitzgerald) 12–13, 14, 22, 24, 110, 121, 122, 166
Great Recession 153
"Great Society" 149
Great War *see* First World War

H

Haitian Revolution 32, 47, 62, 95
Haley, Alex 35
Hamer, Fannie Lou 139
Hamilton, Alexander 9–10, 37, 40, 42–43, 44, 46, 80, 94, 104, 125, 150, 151
Hanchard, Michael 47, 87, 91, 164
Harding, Warren G. 38
Harlan, John Marchal 106, 107–108
Harper's Ferry 90
Hartz, Louis 84
Hathorne, John 18
Hawthorne, Nathaniel 18–19, 71, 72, 75, 87, 90, 91
Hawthorne, Sophia 87, 91
Hayes, Rutherford B. 98, 99–100
health care policy, Obama 159–160
Hegel, G.W.F. 2
Hemings, Robert 33
Hendrix, Jimi 166
Henry, Patrick 38–39, 57, 116
Herndon, William 83
Herrenvolk 53–54, 56, 70

Holmes, John 55
Holocaust, the 19
Homestead Act, 1862 99
hooks, bell 112–113
Horning, Audrey 17
House, Edward M. 117–118
Huebner, Timothy S. 81
Hughes, Langston 95
Hutchinson, Anne 18

I

Idea of Fraternity in America, The
    (McWilliams) 23–24
"identity politics" 121
Illinois 89
immigration: New American State period,
    1877–1932 108–112; Progressive era
    120–121; Trump's policy on 161
Inaugural Address (Trump) 162
incarceration rate, increase in 144
indentured servitude, colonial period
    12, 26
Indian Removal policy 59, 70, 71, 91
Indian Reservations Act 71
Indians *see* indigenous peoples
indigenous peoples: American Revolution
    period 47, 48; and the Articles of
    Confederation 37; colonial period 6,
    10, 12–16, 17, 33; and the
    Declaration of Independence 34, 35;
    forced migration/removal of 59, 70,
    71, 91; genocide policies against 100;
    land management/environmental
    practices 14; New England
    population, c.1600 13; and
    positionality of book 3; Progressive
    era 120–121; and Reconstruction 99;
    rights of 70–71; Tocqueville on 54;
    violence against 89; and the western
    expansion 43, 70
*Indigenous Peoples' History of the United
    States, An* (Dunbar-Ortiz) 14
individuality 25
"inverted totalitarianism" 163
Invisible Man (Ellison) 85, 138
Iraq War 2002 158, 164
Ireland, English colonization of 17

Irish immigrants 109
Islamist terror 97, 154, 158, 162
Italians 107; immigrants 110

J

Jackson, Andrew 59, 60, 70, 83
Jackson, Shirley 19, 20
Jacobson, Matthew Frye 111
James, William 109
James, William, Sr. 112
Jamestown, Virginia settlement, 1607
    11, 12
Japan 115–116
Jefferson, Thomas 10, 33, 44, 45, 56, 61,
    67, 125, 126, 130; Declaration of
    Independence 32, 34; presidency of
    5–6, 45–48, 53, 57–60; radicalism of
    34–35; and slavery 33, 55, 61,
    62, 88
Jewish immigrants 110
Jewish population of Europe 89
Jim Crow 41, 69, 117, 131
John Bowne High School 5
Johnson, Lyndon 132, 141, 149
Joshi, S.T. 68

K

Kael, Pauline 150
Kaledin, Arthur 64
Kansas 82, 90
Kansas-Nebraska Act 74
Katznelson, Ira 4, 31, 126, 129–130
Kendi, Ibram X. 22–23, 66, 131
Kennedy, John F. 97, 142, 153–154, 162
Kennedy, Randall 22
Kennedy, Robert F. 142, 161
Kerber, Linda 65–66
Kim, Claire Jean 68
King, Desmond 63
King, Martin Luther, Jr. 55, 95, 132, 137,
    138, 139, 140–141, 142, 156
King Philip's War, 1675–1676 16, 89
Klinkner, Philip A. 160
Kloppenberg, James T. 119, 155–156
Know Nothings 160

Kramnick, Isaac 110, 118, 137,
142–143, 151

L

labor: need for in colonial period 20, 21;
women's domestic labor in the
colonial period 19, 20; *see also* slavery
labor violence 109
Landynski, Jacob 4
Last of the Mohicans (Cooper) 27, 56, 71
Lebscock, Suzanne 114
Lee, Robert E. 92
Lepore, Jill 15–16, 49, 73, 88, 109,
113, 119
Letter from a Birmingham Jail (King)
137, 138
Leuchtenburg, William E. 136
Lewis, David Levering 113
Lewis, Jan Ellen 61, 62
Liberal Tradition in America, The
(Hartz) 84
Lincoln, Abraham 11, 32, 35, 39, 63, 82,
100, 159; and American democracy
80; assassination of 99; and Civil War
and Reconstruction period 80, 83,
87, 88, 90–91, 92–93, 93–98, 99,
100; Gettysburg Address 10, 38, 40,
82, 86, 94–95, 96–97, 98, 100;
Second Inaugural 82, 84, 88, 94,
95–96, 97, 98, 100; and slavery 54,
60, 61, 74, 80, 83, 87, 88, 90–91
literature, American 3–4
Locke, John 25, 65, 84
Lodge, Henry Cabot 110
"Lottery, The" (Jackson) 19, 20
Louisiana Territory purchase 6, 34, 46,
49, 53, 58–59, 74
Lovejoy, Elijah P. 63
Lowi, Theodore 36, 58, 98, 110, 118,
137, 142–143, 151

M

Maaza, Anika 25
Madden, Fr. Lawrence, SJ 4
Madison, James 37, 40, 44, 45, 89, 94

Magnalia Christi Americana (Mather)
14–15
Malcolm X 1, 2, 140–141, 142,
156, 166
Mann, Charles 14
Mann, Mary 87
Mansfield, Harvey 103
Marilley, Suzanne 113
Marshall, John 59, 70
master-slave dialectic (Hegel) 2
Mather, Cotton 14–15, 16, 22–23
McCain, John 145
McDonald, Forrest 44, 46
McDougall, Walter 17, 25–26, 45
McIntosh, Francis J. 63
McMahon, Kevin 128
McPherson, James 80, 88
McWilliams, Wilson Carey 4, 23–24, 25,
36, 37, 121
Medicaid/Medicare 142
Meese, Edwin 152
Mellow, Nicole 144
Melville, Herman 16, 56–57, 70, 81, 85,
93, 104–105, 121, 166
Menand, Louis 109
Merrill Lynch 153
"Mexicanization of American politics" 73
Mexico: acquisition of territory 69, 116;
war against 54–55, 61, 71, 74, 82,
83, 84
Milkis, Sidney 133
Missouri Compromise, 1820 47, 53, 60,
73, 74, 84
Moby-Dick (Melville) 16, 56–57,
81, 166
Mondale, Walter 144
Morgan, Edmund S. 21
Morone, James A. 15, 16–17, 17–18
Morrison, Toni 115, 165
Mueller Investigation 163
Muhammad, Elijah 140
Myrdal, Gunnar 137

N

National Association for the Advancement
of Colored People 138
National Bank 43

national identity, American 10–11;
    colonial period 27; forging of
    in American Revolution period
    42–45
National Review, The 134, 136, 152
Native Americans *see* indigenous peoples
neoconservatism 7, 145, 150, 158
neoliberalism 7, 161, 164
New American History, A, 1585–1828
    (McDougall) 25–26
New American State period, 1877–1932
    103–105, 121–123; empire and
    democracy 115–119; immigration
    108–112; and *Plessy v. Ferguson*
    106–108; Progressive era 119–121;
    women's rights 112–115
New Deal 7, 31, 121, 125–126, 128,
    132, 134
New Eden myth 12–16
New England 13, 15, 16, 22–23, 91;
    exceptionalism 11–12; Protestants
    10–11
New Federalism 143–144
New Freedom, The (Wilson) 118
"New Left" 144–145
New School for Social Research 4
New York: suffrage rights 111
Newton, Huey P. 28, 34
Niles, H. 32
Nixon, Richard 143–144, 149, 150
non-violent tactics 139
North: American Revolution period
    41; colonial period 11; and
    slavery 91
Northwest Ordinance 37, 54
Norton, Anne 42
Notes on the State of Virginia (Jefferson)
    56, 61, 62, 67, 130

O

Obama, Barack 7, 145, 155–160
"Occupy Wall Street" 104
Ogletree, Charles 133
Ohio Women's Rights Convention,
    1851 67
Oklahoma City bombings 154

"On Civil Disobedience" (Thoreau)
    55, 105
Onuf, Peter S. 61, 62

P

pacifism 139
Paine, Thomas 153
Pan-Africanism 138
Peabody, Elizabeth 87, 91
Peace of Paris 32, 58
People v. Hall (1854) 109
Pequot Indians 16
Perkins, Frances 129
Perry, Matthew 115–116
Pettegrew, John 114, 116, 117
Philippines 117
Phillips, Wendell 99
phrenology 110
Pinto, Joan 5
Pitney, John J. 159
Plato 163
Plessy v. Ferguson (1896) 106, 107–108,
    133
Plymouth, Massachusetts settlement,
    1620 11
Politics and Vision (Wolin) 163–165
Polk, James 44, 83
popular sovereignty 83, 84, 89
populism 119, 126; and Trump
    presidency 161–163
Powell, Colin 158
Prat, Louis H. 139–140
presidency: and the American
    Constitution 41–42, 43; and gender
    41; late state development period 112
Proclamation of Neutrality, 1793 40,
    42, 44
Progressive Era 44, 114, 119–121, 126
Progressive Party 113
Prosser, Gabriel 63
Protestantism: and immigration 109; *see
    also* Puritanism
public school teachers 5
Puerto Rica 117
Puritanism: as foundation for
    American national identity 10;

and the origins of colonial thought 16–20
Putin, Vladimir 154

Q

Quakerism: and non-violent tactics 139; as outsiders in colonial period 17, 18

R

race: and American imperialism 117; American Revolution period 32, 33–36, 40–41, 46–47, 48; and the Articles of Confederation 37; Civil War and Reconstruction period 80–81, 82–89, 90–91, 92, 93, 95, 97, 98, 99, 100; colonial period 12, 20–24; and the Declaration of Independence 35; "Empire of Liberty" period 53–54, 56–57, 61–65, 69–72, 73–74, 75; and Europeans 107; New American State period, 1877–1932 106–113, 117, 120–121, 122–123; positionality of book 2, 3, 6; and presidencies 41; racial demographics, early twenty-first century 160; and rights in the 1932–1980 period 128–129, 131–134, 136–141; and the Trump presidency 160–162
racial segregation 106, 107–108; psychological effect of 133; see also desegregation
racial sex/marriage laws in colonial period 22
racial triangulation 68–69, 108
racism: colonial period 20–21; as consequence of slavery 20; racial formation in colonial period 20–24
Radicalism of the American Revolution, The (Wood) 26, 31
Rakove, Jack 39
Reagan, Ronald 7, 136, 144, 145, 149–151, 152, 153–154, 163
Reconstruction see Civil War and Reconstruction period

religion: and immigration 109; Second Great Awakening 59–60; and slavery 63, 80–81; see also Protestantism; Puritanism
Removal Act, 1830 70
Renan, Ernest 9, 10, 23, 33
"republican motherhood" 65–66
Republican Party 80, 136, 143, 150, 151, 160
republicanism: American Revolution period 32, 42; Anti-Federalist approach to 36
Riley, Russell 43
"Road Not Taken, The" (Frost) 166
Romney, Mitt 160
Roosevelt, Franklin Delano 7, 97, 121, 125–127, 130, 151, 163; and the Second Bill of Rights 127–128
Roosevelt, Theodore 44, 113, 117, 118, 119, 121
Roots (Haley) 35
Royal African Company 25
Rumsfeld, Donald 158
Russell, William 79
Russia: Mueller Investigation 163; see also Soviet Union
Rustin, Bayard 138–139

S

Sainte-Domingue 59, 62
Salem Witch Trials 18
Sanders, Bernie 161
Scandinavians 107
Schall, Fr. James, SJ 4
Schlesinger, Arthur M., Jr. 100
SCLC (Southern Christian Leadership Conference) 138
Scott v. Sanford case see Dred Scott case
Second Bill of Rights 127–128
Second Great Awakening 59–60
Second Inaugural (Lincoln) 82, 84, 88, 94, 95–96, 97, 98, 100
Second Seminole War, 1835–1842 70
Second World War 117, 118, 127
self-help books 25
Seminole Wars, 1816–1819 70
Senate: and slavery 41

Seneca Falls convention 65, 66–67
September 11, 2001 *see* 9/11
Seven Year's War 26
Shay's Rebellion 38, 62
Skowronek, Stephen 108–109
Slack, Charles 45
Slater, James Harvey 109
slavery: American Revolution period 33–35, 40–41, 47, 48; beginnings of in 1619 12; black revolt 61–65, 90; and Christianity 21, 23; Civil War and Reconstruction period 80–81, 82–89, 90–91, 92, 93, 95, 97, 98, 99, 100; colonial period 6, 10, 11, 12, 20–24, 25–26; Emancipation Proclamation 93; "Empire of Liberty" period 53–54, 61–65, 73–74, 75; expansion of into western territories 58, 74, 80, 83, 89, 91, 106; expatriation 55; and the Northwest Ordinance 37; opposition to 54–55, 60; psychological dimension of 64, 69; and religion 59–60; as a southern phenomenon 12; *see also* abolitionist movement
"Slavery as a Positive Good" (Calhoun) 62
Smith, Adam 20
Smith, Rogers 11–12, 35, 41, 46–47, 63, 160
Social Darwinism 106
Song, M.R. 27
Souls of Black Folks, The (Du Bois) 12
South, the: American Revolution period 40–41; colonial period 11, 12; opposition to civil rights 132; racial segregation 106, 107–108; and slavery 11, 12, 62–63, 80
Southeast European immigrants 109
Southern Europeans 107; immigrants 110
Soviet Union 130, 131, 134; collapse of 152–153; US foreign policy towards 150, 152, 158; *see also* Russia
Spanish–American War, 1898 7, 116–117
Spanish colonialism 16
"Speech, The" (Reagan) 149
Stalinism 152

Stamped from the Beginning: The Definitive History of Racist Ideas in America (Kendi) 22–23
Standley, Fred L. 139–140
Stanton, Elizabeth Cady 65, 66–67
Stipelman, Brian 128
Stoler, Ann L. 72
Stowe, Harriet Beecher 66, 72
suffrage rights 111, 112
Suffragist Movement 61
Sumner, Charles 90
superpower, United States as 7, 153–154, 163

T

Taney, Roger B. 74, 86–87, 91, 110
Ten Per Cent Plan 82, 99
terrorism 97, 154, 158
Texas 83
Theweleit, Klans 117
Third Seminole War, 1855–1858 70
"Third Way" 154
Third World 131
Thoreau, Henry David 55, 60, 105
Three-Fifths Compromise 40, 41, 58
Thurmond, Strom 132
Tichenor, Daniel J. 4–5, 110, 113–114, 133
Tilden, Samuel J. 99
Till, Emmett 134
Tocqueville, Alexis de 10–12, 19, 22, 23, 35, 36, 38, 64–65, 68–69, 70–71, 103, 104
Transcendental movement 54, 60–61, 71, 72, 105
Truman, Harry 130, 131–132
Trump, Donald 7, 160–163
Truth, Sojourner 66, 67
Turner, Nat 63

U

University of Virginia 45

V

Van Buren, Martin 71
Vesey, Denmark 63
Vindication of the Government of Churches
    (Wise) 25
Vindication of the Rights of Women
    (Wollstonecraft) 41
Virginia: colonial wars against indigenous
    peoples 15; constitutional ratifying
    convention, 1787 45, 57, 116;
    statute of religious freedom 45
Virginia and Kentucky Resolutions,
    1798 45

W

Wall Street 104, 121
Wallace, George 161
"War on Terror" 118, 154, 158
Washington, DC 74, 104
Washington, George 27, 40, 42; Farewell
    Address 43, 57, 85; influence of
    Hamilton on 42–43; presidency
    42–44
Way to Wealth, The (Franklin) 25
Wayne, Tiffany K. 72
We Were Eight Years in Power (Coates) 98
welfare state: conservative attitudes
    towards 149–150; *see also* health care
    policy, Obama
West, Cornel 156, 165
western expansion 43, 58, 59, 69, 71, 72,
    73, 74, 99
western states 91–92
Whig Party 60, 61, 83
Whiskey Rebellion, 1794 42, 44
white male suffrage 113; expansion of,
    1820s and 1830s 48
White Nationalism 154, 160–163
White, Ronald C. 97
white supremacy 83–84, 85, 106, 107,
    131, 135, 161; American Revolution
    period 32; development of thought in
    Enlightenment period 23–24
white women: American Revolution
    period 41; colonial period 19, 20,

21–22; northern states 91; southern
    states 91; suffrage and political
    rights 113
whiteness 14–15, 21, 110–111
Wilderness Campaign 93
Wilentz, Sean 46, 151
Williams, Eric 20
Williams, Roger 18
Wills, Garry 10, 41, 58, 86, 94
Wilson, Woodrow 98, 112, 117–118,
    120, 121, 126, 159
Wineapple, Brenda 87, 91
Winthrop, Debra 103
Winthrop, John 17, 153
Wise, John 25
Wolfowitz, Paul 158
Wolin, Sheldon 163–165
Wollstonecraft, Mary 41, 66
women 15; American Revolutionary
    period 47; and the Articles of
    Confederation 37; authors 72;
    colonial period 17, 18, 19–20; and
    the Declaration of Independence 35;
    domestic labour of 19–20; "Empire
    of Liberty" period 60–61, 65–70;
    and New Deal policies 129; and
    positionality of book 3, 6; Progressive
    era 120–121; "republican
    motherhood" 65–66; and rights in
    the1932–1980 period 128, 129,
    142–143; scientific arguments,
    eighteenth century 23–24; and
    slavery 66; and Social Darwinism
    106; suffrage and political rights 7,
    55, 65–70, 71–72, 91–92, 99, 100,
    112–115; Tocqueville on 54, 64–65,
    68–69, 70–71; *see also* black women;
    white women
Wood, Gordon 26, 31, 34, 58
Worcester v. Georgia (1832) 70

Y

"Young Goodman Brown" (Hawthorne)
    18–19, 75
Young, James P. 25, 36–37, 39, 40,
    46, 48